REAL
ESTATE
GUIDELINES
AND RULES
OF THUMB

REAL ESTATE GUIDELINES AND RULES OF THUMB

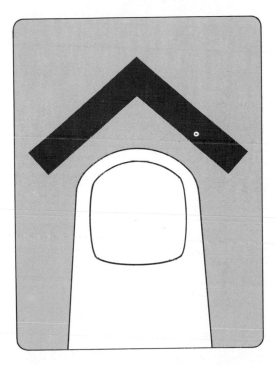

Ronald E. Gettel

MAI, CRE, SREA, ASA

McGraw-Hill Book Company

New York St. Louis San Francisco Auckland
Düsseldorf Johannesburg Kuala Lumpur London
Mexico Montreal New Delhi Panama Paris
São Paulo Singapore Sydney Tokyo Toronto

Library of Congress Cataloging in Publication Data

Gettel, Ronald E   1931–
   Real estate guidelines and rules of thumb.

   Includes index.
   1. Real estate business.   I. Title.
HD1375.G47   333.3'3   76-16125
ISBN 0-07-023173-7

  34567890 **FGFG** 78543210987

The editors for this book were W. Hodson Mogan and Patricia A. Allen,
the designer was Elliot Epstein, and the production supervisor
was Teresa F. Leaden. It was set in Helvetica
by Progressive Typographers.

It was printed and bound by The Kingsport Press.

to
Patti
Lou
Baker
Gettel

Contents

Preface   xi

Author's Note   xiii

PART I   **Site Planning**

  1. 20 percent of land area to streets   3

  2. Lots per acre—I   5

  3. Lots per acre—II   7

  4. How topography influences use   9

  5. Cost of improved lot   12

  6. The 25–50–25 Percent Rule   14

  7. How much you can pay for raw land   26

  8. LUI (land-use intensity) scale   28

  9. How long to hold land   35

10. Ideal maximum distances to daily activities   38

11. The Walk-Away Test   40

12. Nine rules of thumb for off-street parking   43

13. 400 square feet per parking space   45

14. ULI's parking index   46

15. When to build a parking garage   49

16. How many people are needed to support various types
of developments   50

PART II   **Lot Sizes and Shapes**

17. Hoffman Rule   55

18. Hoffman-Neill Rule   56

19. The 4-3-2-1 Rule   58

20. The parabolic formula   60

21. Other depth rules   62

22. Rules for irregular lots   63

23. Rules for corner lots   67

24. Plottage rules   71

PART III Houses and Condominiums

25. 2.5 times annual income — 75

26. One-fourth of income to PITI — 78

27. The Old Rule of 100 — 81

28. The New Rule of 100 — 83

29. Sale prices of condominium units vs. values as apartments — 85

30. Margins for condominium conversions — 87

31. Apartments best suited for conversion — 88

32. The best time to buy a home — 91

PART IV Income Properties

33. Future, the tense that counts — 97

34. Most important future: The near future — 98

35. No. 1 goal of many: Cash flow — 104

36. Loan rates related to bond yields — 107

37. Loan interest rate vs. payment size as value determinant — 110

38. Loan rates related to property types — 117

39. Debt coverage factors — 121

40. Real property values related to general rate movements — 124

41. Real estate yields related to the prime rate — 127

42. Proper capitalization rates and methods — 128

43. Unsound methods, including Built-Up Method — 130

44. Band of Investment Method — 132

45. More suitable methods (McLaughlin, Ellwood, Johnson) — 134

46. Gettel's Method — 136

47. How long a mortgage loan term is acceptable to lenders—I — 141

48. How long a mortgage loan term is acceptable to lenders—II — 144

49. Formula for maximum rent for "blue chip" tenants — 148

50. Typical operating percentages for apartments — 150

51. Typical operating percentages for major office buildings — 153

52. Typical operating percentages for shopping centers — 155

53. Typical operating percentages for motels — 159

54. Typical operating percentages for major hotels and
motor hotels   163

55. Typical percentage rents   171

56. $1/gallon/month for service stations   182

57. Types of stores suitable for particular types
of locations   184

PART V   Potpourri

58. How to tell real estate from personal property   191

59. Assessed value vs. market value   194

60. Farm values per acre   195

61. Useful lives of buildings   210

62. Depreciation tables   214

63. The CPI (Consumer Price Index) as a tool for real
estate people   217

64. Developing your own rules of thumb   221

65. The best investment in real estate   225

Index   231

Preface

RULES OF THUMB: BOON OR BANE?

Caution: Using rules of thumb can be risky.

> *Generalizations are generally wrong.**
> —MARY WORTLEY MONTAGU

Some—but far from all—of the chapters in this book deal with rules of thumb.

Real estate professionals and students alike are keenly interested in rules of thumb. In meetings and classes, note pads come out at the drop of a rule of thumb.

"Will you repeat that part about the rule of 100?" "Why *isn't* it all right to rely on the 4-3-2-1 Rule?" "Is it safe to allow 20 percent of a tract for streets?" "Do capitalization rates change every time prime rates do?" And so on, and on.

Yet you don't see much about rules of thumb in our leading textbooks. You don't hear much about rules of thumb in our professional appraisal courses. Why? These seem to be the main reasons:

1. Rules of thumb can be misused. Tell lazy or less-than-able people about rules of thumb and they are apt to use them without understanding and proper restraint.

2. Just as there are no two fingerprints exactly alike, there are no parcels of real estate exactly alike; every real property is *unique.* Yet every rule of thumb is a generalization.

3. Real estate markets are *dynamic;* they change—sometimes quite radically —over time. Using a capitalization rate that would have been suitable in 1974 might lead to a ridiculous conclusion in 1981.

4. In the real estate appraisal field and in other branches of real estate, we've been developing—and are still refining and improving—a professional methodology and discipline to protect and otherwise help our clients. Surely, no thinking professional seriously wants to retreat to just the use of rules of thumb, averages, and guidelines.

   A rule of thumb, no matter how soundly based, will not take the place of detailed analysis in a specific case. Perhaps this is the most telling argument against the ill-informed use of rules of thumb: "You shouldn't use a rule of thumb unless you have enough data to support it, and you don't need the rule of thumb if you have that much market data."

---

* Presumably, this was meant as a *generalization.*

Yet an understanding of rules of thumb is essential to the real estate professional.

> My mind seems to have become a kind of machine for grinding general laws out of large collections of facts.
>
> —CHARLES DARWIN

The arguments above are very persuasive arguments for limited and prudent use of rules of thumb. They are not good reasons for rejecting them out of hand. Consider:

1. Other tools of real estate professionals—automobiles, calculators, and sales data, to name a few—can be terribly misused, but we don't seriously consider doing without them.

   Because they can be used well and can be very helpful. So can rules of thumb.

2. Generalizations are always risky, but generalizations which are based upon knowledge of a field are useful—indeed, absolutely necessary—in every field of human endeavor. Especially since he deals with a very heterogeneous and changing commodity, the quintessential real estate professional is always seeking reasonable points of central tendency. To the extent that it tends to represent a common denominator for a varying commodity—generalization can be very valuable.

3. Real estate markets are dynamic, but rules of thumb tend to persist. Some have shown incredible durability. A few of the best known and most-used real estate rules of thumb are older than any real estate professional now living. Out-of-date rules of thumb should be recognized as such. Hopefully, this book will help.

4. A real estate professional functions in the real world. To refuse to study rules of thumb would be to turn one's back on tools used by tens of thousands of people every year—people who heavily influence the value of real estate.

   How many assessors use depth tables? How many lenders rely on certain debt coverage ratios? How many shopping center developers rely on certain parking ratios? How many site planners are guided by LUI standards? How many . . .

Certainly, tens of thousands of important real estate decisions are made annually which involve some reliance on real estate rules of thumb.

Some are good tools.

Some are bad tools.

But they *are* used.

Author's Note

If a little knowledge is dangerous, where is the man who has so much as to be out of danger?

—T. H. HUXLEY

Limitations. This book was prepared with great care so that it can be of important benefit to the reader. However, certain limitations should be noted:

- It seems reasonable to believe that, somewhere in the thousands of numbers and tens of thousands of words, some error has crept in. Absolute accuracy is not assured.

- Not all guidelines and rules of thumb in the real estate field are included. Far from it. Each one treated in this book was selected because it is in widespread use or has some important validity which can be demonstrated, or both.

REAL ESTATE GUIDELINES AND RULES OF THUMB

Part I

Site
Planning

No man acquires property without acquiring with it a little arithmetic also.
—EMERSON

1 20 percent of land area to streets

A popular rule of thumb: In preliminary planning for a large residential subdivision, allocate 20 percent or so of the gross land area to streets.

However, even in preliminary work, one must be aware of the exceptions to this "rule" and the range of variations.

Suppose you are looking at a 100-acre tract. You know it is well suited for a residential subdivision. Its shape is good. Its topography is fairly level. From your experience in the area, you know that an optimum layout will involve lot depths of 150 feet or so, blocks averaging about 750 feet in length, and 50-foot-wide streets. In your preliminary plan, you assume that 20 percent or 20 acres will be needed for streets.

Are you right? You are—in this case.

A 20 percent allowance for streets is probably a reasonable point of central tendency. However, in certain cases, streets may require from less than 15 percent to more than 30 percent. Small land area, awkward shape, unusual requirements by governmental agencies, atypical lot layouts—these and other factors can lead to important deviations from the 20 percent figure.

On the next page is a table that can be used for preliminary planning of subdivisions of various types, including subdivisions for detached dwellings, PUDs (planned unit developments), and mobile-home parks.

There is really no need to use the 20 percent figure; more accurate estimates like those included in this table can be prepared in minutes.

HOW MUCH OF THE TRACT IS NEEDED FOR STREETS?

Average street width, ft.	Average block length, ft.	Average lot depth, ft.	Percent of land needed for streets
		100	22.8
	500	125	20.2
		150	18.3
		200	15.8
		100	20.9
40	750	125	18.2
		150	16.2
		200	13.7
		100	19.9
	1,000	125	17.1
		150	15.2
		200	12.6
		100	27.3
	500	125	24.2
		150	22.1
		200	19.2
		100	25.0
50	750	125	21.9
		150	19.6
		200	16.7
		100	23.9
	1,000	125	20.6
		150	18.4
		200	15.4
		100	31.3
	500	125	28.0
		150	25.6
		200	22.4
		100	28.8
60	750	125	25.3
		150	22.8
		200	19.5
		100	27.4
	1,000	125	23.9
		150	21.1
		200	18.0

2   Lots per acre—I

How many salable lots will a tract yield? This table will help you find the answer.

This simple table can be helpful, but it will not take the place of experience and judgment. Any answer will be only as good as the judgment used in selecting the best average lot size and an appropriate allowance for open space.

HOW MANY LOTS PER GROSS ACRE?

Average lot size, sq. ft.	Percentage of open space in streets and parks:						
	20%	25%	30%	35%	40%	45%	50%
2,000	17.4	16.3	15.2	14.2	13.1	12.0	10.9
3,000	11.6	10.9	10.2	9.4	8.7	8.0	7.3
4,000	8.7	8.2	7.6	7.1	6.5	6.0	5.4
5,000	7.0	6.5	6.1	5.7	5.2	4.8	4.4
6,000	5.8	5.4	5.1	4.7	4.4	4.0	3.6
7,000	5.0	4.7	4.4	4.0	3.7	3.4	3.1
8,000	4.4	4.1	3.8	3.5	3.3	3.0	2.7
9,000	3.9	3.6	3.4	3.1	2.9	2.7	2.4
10,000	3.5	3.3	**3.0**	2.8	2.6	2.4	2.2
11,000	3.2	3.0	2.8	2.6	2.4	2.2	2.0
12,000	2.9	2.7	2.5	2.4	2.2	2.0	1.8
13,000	2.7	2.5	2.3	2.2	2.0	1.8	1.7
14,000	2.5	2.3	2.2	2.0	1.9	1.7	1.6
15,000	2.3	2.2	2.0	1.9	1.7	1.6	1.5
16,000	2.2	2.0	1.9	1.8	1.6	1.5	1.4
20,000	1.7	1.6	1.5	1.4	1.3	1.2	1.1
25,000	1.4	1.3	1.2	1.1	1.0	1.0	0.9
30,000	1.2	1.1	1.0	0.9	0.9	0.8	0.7
35,000	1.0	0.9	0.9	0.8	0.7	0.7	0.6
40,000	0.9	0.8	0.8	0.7	0.7	0.6	0.5

Example: In the example indicated, the developer assumed a typical lot size of 10,000 sq. ft. (say 80 × 125 ft.) and that 30% of the gross land area will be committed to public rights-of-way and to private recreational use; the yield will be approximately three salable lots per gross acre.

3 Lots per acre—II

How many salable lots will a tract yield? Here's a diagram that does about the same thing as the table on the preceding page.

HOW MANY LOTS PER GROSS ACRE?

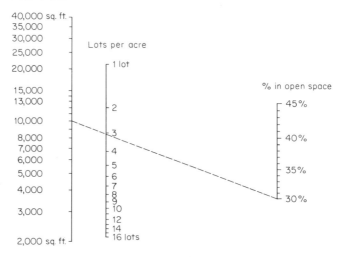

How many lots per gross acre?

Note: Select appropriate points on the two outside scales, and lay a straightedge between them. The point at which the straightedge intersects the middle scale indicates the approximate number of salable lots per gross acre.

Example: If 30% of the gross land area is to be in open space and the average lot size is to be 10,000 square feet, then the subdivision plan will yield approximately 3 lots per gross acre.

4 How topography influences use

A site's topography can have much to do with what that site should be used for.

On the next two pages are useful general guidelines.

Costs of changing the slopes on a site—grading, excavating, use of grade-changing devices—can be a major part of the development cost.

One way of keeping these costs to a minimum is to match slopes and uses.

Opinions vary somewhat from one planning expert to another, but the guidelines set out on the next page are fairly typical. One may depart from these guidelines if sites are so well located and so valuable that higher site-preparation costs and more costly construction techniques are warranted.

Getting a topographic survey of a tract you are interested in may be a very wise preliminary step. Two sources of data that may help you evaluate the general topography of a tract are the Department of Interior (U.S. Geological Survey) and the Department of Agriculture (Soil Surveys).

TOPOGRAPHY RELATED TO SITE DEVELOPMENT

Average percent of slope	Use potential
0–1	Good for building sites, parking lots, roads, and recreation—if certain site-improvement problems can be solved.
1–7	Good for building sites, parking lots, roads, and recreation.
7–20	Fair for building sites and roads. Difficult for parking lots and recreation.
Over 20	Open-space (conservation, buffer) uses.

Comments

Very flat land can present serious problems in sewage and storm drainage, problems that are costly to solve.

Limited need for grade-changing devices and excavation for development. May be particularly advantageous if general gradual slope down to sewer lines.

Gently sloping land usually more physically attractive than flat land for residential development.

6 or 7% generally considered maximum ideal slope for parking lots. On sloping land, the maximum ideal distance for patrons to walk from parking spaces is lessened for the simple reason that people don't like to walk uphill. Another consideration is whether shopping carts will roll into the street or into cars—especially if aided by a wind.

Some motorists are less inclined to enter service stations and other properties if entry drives look steep.

Very uneven topography can provide interesting homesites; but unless building designs are adapted to uneven terrain, more costly construction and/or excavation will be needed.

Steep slopes can be made into spectacular homesites, but development costs are usually extreme.

Cost of improved lot

This scale can help the reader find the development cost of a lot (raw land and street improvements only).

Here again, this helpful scale for computing certain lot costs is based solely on simple arithmetic. Judgment factors are left to the reader who uses it.

COMPUTING CHART
TO FIND THE TOTAL COST OF AN IMPROVED LOT
(RAW LAND AND STREET IMPROVEMENTS)

COST OF STREET IMPROVEMENTS DOLLARS PER FRONT FOOT — SCALE B

COST OF RAW LAND DOLLARS PER ACRE — SCALE A

TOTAL COST - DOLLARS PER LOT INCLUDING RAW LAND & STREET IMPROVEMENTS

100' X 200' SCALE F — 70' X 140' SCALE E — 60' X 120' SCALE C — 70' X 100' SCALE D

— NOTE —

IN THIS CHART APPROXIMATELY 30% OF THE GROSS ACREAGE IS ALLOWED FOR PUBLICLY DEDICATED LAND.

LOT SIZE	NET LOTS PER ACRE
60' X 120'	4.2
70' X 100'	4.3
70' X 140'	3.1
100' X 200'	1.5

IN ARRIVING AT THE TOTAL COST OF EACH IMPROVED LOT AN ALLOWANCE MUST BE ADDED TO THE FRONT FOOT COST FOR THE INSTALLATION OF IMPROVEMENTS IN THE CROSS STREETS OF WHICH NO LOTS FACE. THIS ALLOWANCE WILL VARY FROM 12% TO 40% DEPENDING ON THE LENGTH AND WIDTH OF BLOCKS.

AN ADDITIONAL ALLOWANCE FOR RAW LAND COST SHOULD BE MADE WHERE LARGE PARK AREAS ARE DEDICATED.

— INSTRUCTIONS —

LAY STRAIGHT EDGE ACROSS SCALES "A," "B," "C," "D," "E" AND "F" SO THAT IT CROSSES SCALE "A" AT THE POINT REPRESENTING THE COST OF RAW LAND PER ACRE, AND CROSSES SCALE "B" AT THE POINT REPRESENTING THE COST OF STREET IMPROVEMENTS PER FRONT FOOT. THE READING AT THE POINT WHERE THE STRAIGHT EDGE CROSSES SCALE "D" INDICATES THE TOTAL COST OF AN IMPROVED 70 FT. BY 100 FT. LOT; WHERE THE STRAIGHT EDGE CROSSES SCALE "C" INDICATES THE TOTAL COST OF AN IMPROVED 60 FT. BY 120 FT. LOT; WHERE THE STRAIGHT EDGE CROSSES SCALE "E" INDICATES THE TOTAL COST OF AN IMPROVED 70 FT. BY 140 FT. LOT; WHERE THE STRAIGHT EDGE CROSSES SCALE "F"; INDICATES THE TOTAL COST OF AN IMPROVED 100 FT. BY 200 FT. LOT.

EXAMPLE: WHERE THE COST OF RAW LAND IS $1,800 PER ACRE, AND THE REQUIRED IMPROVEMENTS COST $14 PER FRONT FOOT. PLACE THE STRAIGHT EDGE ON SCALE "A" AT $1,800 AND SCALE "B" AT $14.

FOR 4.2 LOTS PER ACRE - 60' X 120' - READ ON SCALE "C" $1,270, THE COST OF AN IMPROVED LOT.

FOR 4.3 LOTS PER ACRE - 70' X 100' - READ ON SCALE "D" $1,400, THE COST OF AN IMPROVED LOT.

FOR 3.1 LOTS PER ACRE - 70' X 140' - READ ON SCALE "E" $1,560, THE COST OF AN IMPROVED LOT.

FOR 1.5 LOTS PER ACRE - 100' X 200' - READ ON SCALE "F" $2,600, THE COST OF AN IMPROVED LOT.

Source: Federal Housing Administration.

6 The 25-50-25 Percent Rule

The 25-50-25 Percent Rule: This rule holds that the costs of developing raw acreages into residential subdivisions are typically:

Cost of Raw Land	**25%**
Development, Administrative, Sales, and Carrying Costs	**50**
Developer's Profit	**25**
Selling Prices of Lots	**100%**

This rule of thumb has some basis in experience, but it certainly doesn't apply in all cases.

Actual experience in many subdivisions has been roughly consistent with this breakdown.

However, actual experience in many other instances has been far different from this.

There are so many variables that it can be disastrous to rely on this rule of thumb—or on one of the similar rules of thumb about subdivision development costs. Consider:

1. Subdivision design features and off-site improvements can vary radically. Will there be paved streets? Curbs? Walks? Streetlights? Public water? Sewers? Private park areas?

2. Even with similar layouts and similar off-site improvements, development costs can vary substantially. In some areas, public entities install off-site improvements and charge the developer only a fraction of the cost. Further, costs of getting the same work done can vary importantly from one area to another.

3. Differences in the sell-out period can be important. Promotion, sales, and carrying costs may be much less for a subdivision that will sell out in two years than for one which will require eight years.

4. To some extent, cost items can be transferred from one category to another. If in negotiating for purchase of undeveloped land, a developer agrees to pay a higher sale price but gets the seller to agree to a lower interest rate on the contract balance, land cost goes up, and carrying costs go down. A utility-line assessment might be classified as a land cost or as a development cost, depending on whether it is borne by the seller of the land or by the purchaser-developer.

A cardinal rule of land developers: Don't put the money in until you have to. This does not refer to limiting quality but rather recognizes the importance of timing.

Thousands of attractive subdivisions have failed financially because their developers made assumptions about the timing of investments and cash flow which didn't
work out. (The importance of timing and cash flow are discussed in more detail in
several chapters in Part IV.)

On the following pages is a projection for a subdivision development which illustrates very well the importance of timing and cash flow. This is an actual projection
modified only so that the identity of the developer and subdivision will not be
apparent. This example is neither especially typical nor particularly unusual. In this
example, the breakdown of costs is approximately:

Cost of Raw Land	$ 220,000	(21%)
Development, Carrying, and Sales Costs	563,694	(54)
Developer's Profit	225,506	(25)
Selling Prices of Lots	$1,039,200	(100%)

Note that the developer's initial capital outlay of $10,000 is extremely small, equiv-
alent to only 1 percent of the projected lot sales. If all goes according to the projection, the developer's reward will be almost $180,000 in the fourth year. The
substantial difference is not imputable to profit alone. During the four-year
period, this experienced developer will have worked long and hard without salary.

One can make sound arguments for stating the developer's profit allowances as
a percentage of investment rather than as a percentage of the retail value of the
lots.

Fortunes have been made via the subdivision development route. Fortunes have
also been lost along the same avenue. The costs, the rewards, the risks—all are
much too great for the developer to depend on such rules of thumb as this.

LAKESIDE DEVELOPMENT
(A PROPOSED PARTNERSHIP
TO DEVELOP LAKESIDE ADDITION)

Projected Financial Statements, Four-Year Period

OPERATING ASSUMPTIONS

(1) Operations:
    (a) Lakeside Development (a proposed partnership) will operate as a land developer of real estate consisting of approximately 100 acres at the edge of Omaha.

    (b) The developed real estate will consist of 86 residential lots from five sections.

    (c) The proposed selling price of each lot will be as follows:

Section	Number of lots	Sale price per lot
I	21	$10,950
II	17	12,450
III	18	12,450
IV	14	12,450
V	16	12,450

    (d) Anticipated sales from each section during the four-year projected period are as follows and on the following terms:

Year of sale	Section	Number of lot sales For cash	Number of lot sales On contract	Projected sales Cash	Projected sales Contract	Total
1977	I	7	7	76,650	$ 76,650	$153,300
1978	I & II	12	12	143,400	144,900	288,300
1979	III & IV	12	12	149,400	149,400	298,800
1980	IV & V	12	12	149,400	149,400	298,800

(2) Cost of Lot Sales:
    (a) The cost of the land and the development expenditures are estimated to be $627,300. This amount divided by the total number of lots in all of the sections (86) results in an approximate per lot cost of $7,294.

    (b) The amounts making up the total cost of $627,300 are as follows:

Land (approximately 100 acres)	$220,000
Sewer assessment (100 acres @ $535)	53,500
Sewer line (9,500 ft. @ $6.50 plus lift station plus contingencies)	100,000
Road costs (first four sections—$20 per ft; fifth section—$18 per ft.)	188,000
Engineering (complete—averaging approximately $230 per lot)	19,800
Storm drainage	11,000
Grass and cleanup	7,000
Entrances (2)	6,000
Lake (lake—2 acres; park—4 acres; landscaping)	22,000
	$627,300

(3) Operating Expenses: Operating expenses during each of the four years are projected as follows:

	1977	1978	1979	1980
Sales commissions	$ 7,665	$14,415	$14,940	$14,940
Advertising and promotion	3,000	1,000	1,000	2,000
Auto expenses	600	600	600	600
Closing costs	2,100	3,600	3,600	3,600
Dues and subscriptions	100	100	100	100
Insurance	100	100	100	100
Legal and accounting fees	1,200	1,200	1,200	1,200
Licenses and permits	50	50	50	50
Office supplies and expenses	600	600	600	600
Taxes—property	1,200	1,500	1,200	900
Travel expenses	200	200	200	200
Miscellaneous	1,200	1,200	1,200	1,200
	$18,015	$24,565	$24,790	$25,490

(4) Interest Received: Interest income is derived from the sale of lots on contract. The assumed rate is 8%. For purposes of this projection, the interest on contracts receivable is recognized as income in the year in which it is collected.

(5) Interest Expense:

    (a) Total borrowings on a real estate first mortgage loan will amount to $300,000 during 1977 and 1978. The interest rate of 10% is computed on the unpaid balance. The term of the loan will be based on the frequency of lot sales collections.

    (b) The seller of the land has agreed to accept a second mortgage on the real estate in the amount of $35,000, interest at the rate of 8% on the unpaid balance. The term of the loan will be for three years starting March 1, 1977.

    (c) Annual interest charges for each of the projected four years are as follows:

Year	First mortgage	Second mortgage	Total
1977	$17,792	$1,890	$19,682
1978	22,000	1,751	23,751
1979	15,500	802	16,302
1980	3,750	49	3,799

(6) Federal and State Income Taxes: No provision has been made for federal and state income taxes payable inasmuch as such taxes are obligations of the individual partners. Also, no provision has been made for partner withdrawals to cover the individual partners' income tax liability resulting from the partnership.

FINANCIAL-CONDITION ASSUMPTIONS

(7) Contracts Receivable:

    (a) It is anticipated that one-half of the lots will be sold on a contract basis with approximately 25% as a down payment and the remainder in three semiannual installments, together with interest at the rate of 8% per annum on the unpaid balance.

    (b) The cash flow from a typical contract for a $10,950 sale and a $12,450 sale is shown below:

	Total payment	Applied to Interest	Applied to Principal	Principal balance
Sale price				$10,950
Down payment	$2,550		$2,550	8,400
6 months later	3,136	$336	2,800	5,600
12 months later	3,024	224	2,800	2,800
18 months later	2,912	112	2,800	

	Total payment	Applied to Interest	Applied to Principal	Principal balance
Sale Price				$12,450
Down payment	$3,150		$3,150	9,300
6 months later	3,472	$372	3,100	6,200
12 months later	3,348	248	3,100	3,100
18 months later	3,224	124	3,100	

(8) Accounts Payable: Accounts payable will be equal to approximately one-twelfth of the annual amount of developmental costs and operating expenses incurred.

(9) Estimated Costs to Complete Development: The procedure of recording a provision for estimated costs required to complete the development of real estate lots permits the matching of costs and related revenues in the proper operating periods and recognizes the company's obligation to complete the required work on real estate available for sale.

(10) First Mortgage Notes: The anticipated cash flow resulting from the first mortgage notes is shown below:

	Total payments	10% interest	Principal additions (deductions)	Principal balance
3/1/77 Initial loan			$185,000	$185,000
6/1/77 Additional loan			15,000	200,000
6/30/77 Interest payment to 6/30/77	$6,292	$6,292		200,000
7/1/77 Additional loan			40,000	240,000
9/30/77 Interest payment to 9/30/77	6,000	6,000		240,000
9/30/77 Lot payoffs (4 @ 5,000)	20,000		(20,000)	220,000
12/31/77 Interest payment to 12/31/77	5,500	5,500		220,000
12/31/77 Lot payoffs (3 @ 5,000)	15,000		(15,000)	205,000
3/31/78 Interest payment to 3/31/78	5,125	5,125		205,000
3/31/78 Lot payoffs (3 @ 5,000)	15,000		(15,000)	190,000
4/1/78 Additional loan			30,000	220,000
6/30/78 Interest payment to 6/30/78	5,500	5,500		220,000
6/30/78 Lot payoffs (3 @ 5,000)	15,000		(15,000)	205,000
7/1/78 Additional loan			30,000	235,000
9/30/78 Interest payment to 9/30/78	5,875	5,875		235,000
9/30/78 Lot payoffs (3 @ 5,000)	15,000		(15,000)	220,000
12/31/78 Interest payment to 12/31/78	5,500	5,500		220,000
12/31/78 Lot payoffs (4 @ 5,000)	20,000		(20,000)	200,000
3/31/79 Interest payment to 3/31/79		5,000		200,000
3/31/79 Lot payoffs (6 @ 5,000)	30,000		(30,000)	170,000
6/30/79 Interest payment to 6/30/79		4,250		170,000
6/30/79 Lot payoffs (6 @ 5,000)	30,000		(30,000)	140,000
9/30/79 Interest payment to 9/30/79		3,500		140,000
9/30/79 Lot payoffs (6 @ 5,000)	30,000		(30,000)	110,000
12/31/79 Interest payment to 12/31/79		2,750		110,000
12/31/79 Lot payoffs (6 @ 5,000)	30,000		(30,000)	80,000
3/31/80 Interest payment to 3/31/80		2,000		80,000
3/31/80 Lot payoffs (6 @ 5,000)	30,000		(30,000)	50,000
6/30/80 Interest payment to 6/30/80		1,250		50,000
6/30/80 Lot payoffs (6 @ 5,000)	30,000		(30,000)	20,000
9/30/80 Interest payment to 9/30/80		500		20,000
9/30/80 Lot payoffs (final)	20,000		(20,000)	

(11) Second Mortgage Note: Cash requirements for the second mortgage note are shown below:

	Total payment	Applied to Interest (8%)	Applied to Principal	Principal balance
3/1/77				$35,000
4/1/77 to 12/1/77 (9 payments @ 1,097)	$ 9,873	$1,890	$ 7,983	27,017
1/1/78 to 12/1/78 (12 payments @ 1,097)	13,164	1,751	11,413	15,604
1/1/79 to 12/1/79 (12 payments @ 1,097)	13,164	802	12,362	3,242
1/1/80 to 3/1/80 (3 payments @ 1,097)	3,291	49	3,242	

(12) Partners' Equity: The initial capital contribution of $10,000 by the partners will be made during January 1977.

LAKESIDE DEVELOPMENT
(A PROPOSED PARTNERSHIP)
EXHIBIT A

Four-Year Projected Statement of Operations
and Capital

Assumption reference code		Operating year			
		1977	1978	1979	1980
1	Lot Sales	$153,300	$288,300	$298,800	$298,800
2 (a)	Cost of Sales	97,580	167,280	167,280	167,280
	Gross Profit on Sales	$ 55,720	$121,020	$131,520	$131,520
3	Operating Expenses	18,015	24,565	24,790	25,490
	Operating Income	$ 37,705	$ 96,455	$106,730	$106,030
4, 7	Other Income—Interest Received	336	5,820	8,748	8,928
		$ 38,041	$102,275	$115,478	$114,958
5, 9, 10	Other Expenses—Interest Expense	19,682	23,751	16,302	3,799
6	Net Income	$ 18,359	$ 78,524	$ 99,176	$111,159
12	Partners' Capital, Beginning of Year	10,000	28,359	106,883	206,059
12	Partners' Capital, End of Year	$ 28,359	$106,883	$206,059	$317,218

LAKESIDE DEVELOPMENT
(A PROPOSED PARTNERSHIP)
EXHIBIT B

Four-Year Projected Statement of Financial
Condition

Assumption reference code		At end of year			
		1977	1978	1979	1980
ASSETS:					
	Cash—Exhibit C	$ 9,206	$ 42,847	$ 2,291	$179,838
7	Contracts receivable	56,000	108,000	111,600	111,600
2 (b)	Inventory—land and development costs (Original cost—$627,300 less lots costed out at $6,970 each)	529,720	362,440	195,160	27,880
		$594,926	$513,287	$309,051	$319,318
LIABILITIES AND CAPITAL:					
8	Accounts payable	$ 8,250	$ 14,500	$ 19,750	$ 2,100
9	Estimated costs to complete development	326,300	176,300		
10	First mortgage notes	205,000	200,000	80,000	
11	Second mortgage note	27,017	15,604	3,242	
		$566,567	$406,404	$102,992	$ 2,100
12	Partners' equity	28,359	106,883	206,059	317,218
		$594,926	$513,287	$309,051	$319,318

LAKESIDE DEVELOPMENT
(A PROPOSED PARTNERSHIP)

EXHIBIT C

Four-Year Projected Statement of Cash Flow

Assumption reference code		Operating Year			
		1977	1978	1979	1980
	Cash Balance, Beginning of Year		$ 9,206	$ 42,847	$ 2,291
SOURCE OF FUNDS:					
12	Initial capital contribution	$ 10,000			
7 (a)	Sales and contract collections:				
7 (b)	Principal	97,300	236,300	295,200	298,800
4, 7 (b)	Interest	336	5,820	8,748	8,928
10	Loan proceeds	240,000	60,000		
	Funds Available	$347,636	$311,326	$346,795	$310,019
REQUIREMENTS FOR FUNDS:					
2 (b), 5 (b)	Land (Cost—$220,000 less second mortgage $35,000)	$185,000			
2 (b)	Development costs	81,000	150,000	176,300	
3	Operating expenses	18,015	24,565	24,790	25,490
8	Decrease (increase) in accounts payable	(8,250)	(6,250)	(5,250)	17,650
		$275,765	$168,315	$195,840	$ 43,140
10	First mortgage loan	35,000	65,000	120,000	80,000
11	Second mortgage loan	7,983	11,413	12,362	3,242
5, 10	Interest—First mortgage loan	17,792	22,000	15,500	3,750
5, 11	Interest—Second mortgage loan	1,890	1,751	802	49
		$338,430	$268,479	$344,504	$130,181
	Cash Balance, End of Year —Exhibit B	$ 9,206	42,847	$ 2,291	$179,838

 How much you can pay for raw land

How much can you afford to pay for undeveloped land for a residential subdivision, an office park, or an industrial park? Here is an interesting table that can help you find the answer.

As we saw in the preceding chapter, timing and cash flow are of vital importance to land developers. How much of the total outlay must be paid out initially? When will other costs be incurred and in what amounts? How much will lot sales yield, and when? The wise developer requires answers to these questions before deciding how much he can afford to pay for an undeveloped tract.

Assuming that one expects lot sales and additional costs to be about the same each year it will take to develop and sell out the project, then this table can be used to decide how much to spend for raw land *as a percentage of anticipated lot prices.*

If, however, the developer anticipates sizable variations in lot sales or in the additional costs from year to year, or if other assumptions are different from those in this table, appropriate "custom" calculations can readily be made by the skilled real estate counselor.

Assumptions: Sales are made in equal annual amounts (as percent of aggregate retail value of lots); after initial investment, costs are incurred in equal annual amounts; all on year-end basis.

Example: You are considering buying and subdividing a tract which will yield (100 lots @ $4,000) $400,000. You can gain control of this raw land and get the development under way with an original cash outlay of $40,000 (10% of retail value). You anticipate that the 100 lots can be sold off in 5 years, with about the same number of lots being sold each year. You estimate additional costs, including a fair profit for you, at $200,000 (50% of retail), and that these additional costs will be incurred in fairly even amounts over the next 5 years. You know that a speculative interest rate fairly reflecting investment factors in this particular case would be on the order of 10%. What can you afford to pay for this raw land based on your assumptions? According to the table: 28% of $400,000 = $112,000.

HOW MUCH OF ANTICIPATED LOT PRICES (RETAIL VALUE) CAN YOU AFFORD TO SPEND FOR RAW LAND?

Level Annual Premise, Various Speculative Interest Rates

Initial cash investment (% of retail)	All of future cost including profit allowance (% of retail)	Value of raw land (as % of retail value) if developed in:								
		5 years			10 years			15 years		
		Cash flow discounted to present worth at rate of			Cash flow discounted to present worth at rate of			Cash flow discounted to present worth at rate of		
		8%	10%	12%	8%	10%	12%	8%	10%	12%
5	20	59	56	53	49	44	40	41	36	31
	30	51	40	46	42	38	34	35	31	27
	40	43	41	38	35	32	29	29	25	22
	50	35	33	31	28	26	23	24	20	18
	60	27	25	24	21	20	18	18	15	13
10	20	54	51	48	44	39	35	36	31	26
	30	46	43	41	37	33	29	30	26	22
	40	38	36	33	30	27	24	24	20	17
	50	30	**28**	26	23	21	18	19	15	13
	60	22	20	19	16	15	13	13	10	8
15	20	49	46	43	39	34	30	31	26	21
	30	41	38	36	32	28	24	25	21	17
	40	33	31	28	25	22	19	19	15	12
	50	25	23	21	18	16	13	14	10	8
	60	17	15	14	11	10	8	8	5	3
20	20	44	41	38	34	29	25	26	21	16
	30	36	33	31	27	23	19	20	16	12
	40	28	26	23	20	17	14	14	10	7
	50	20	18	16	13	11	8	9	5	3
	60	12	10	9	6	5	3	3		

When we think and talk about residential density and land-use intensity, it's usually in fairly simple terms.

However, the land-use-intensity scale goes further.

Several years ago, the Federal Housing Administration (FHA) faced up to some facts.

It wasn't enough to set standards for residential density (the number of dwelling units per acre). Dwellings can vary so much in size and in the number of occupants per unit that density may not be at all consistent with *intensity* of use.

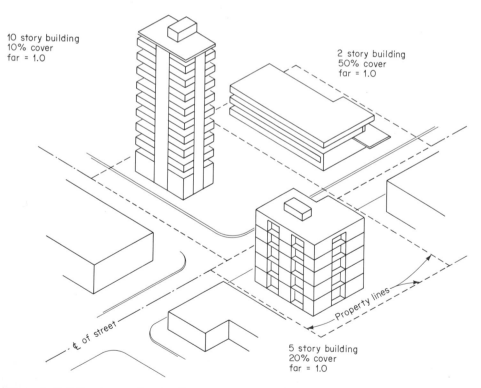

Figure A. Building types related to floor area ratios (FAR). (A floor area ratio of 1.0 or 1.1 simply means that the floor area of the building—the total area on all levels—is equal to the land area. All three structures pictured here have the same floor area ratio, but their building-to-land ratios are very different.) *Source:* U.S. Department of Housing and Urban Development—Federal Housing Administration

And it didn't seem to be enough to set a *simple* standard for land-use *intensity* (the ratio of floor area to land area). For any given land-use intensity, building designs can vary radically as shown in Figure A. As building designs vary, so may some other factors.

The knowledgeable designer of an apartment, condominium, cooperative, or other planned unit development (PUD) structure is not just interested in the floor area ratio; he knows that other building-to-land relationships are very important too. How much open space should there be? How much open space will be free of autos? How much recreation space? How many parking spaces for each living unit?

Appropriate answers to these questions vary from one type of location to another and from one level of land-use intensity to another. In a suburban setting with modest density and moderate land prices, the open space ratio will normally be relatively high. In a central location with high unit land values and much high-rise construction, lower open space ratios are considered acceptable.

So, to help apply better standards of land-use intensity, FHA drew up the land-use-intensity scale reproduced on page 30. About its use, FHA explains:

> In essence the FHA, by assigning its intensity rating to a site, ascribes to the site a selected set of land-use standards consisting of maximum floor area ratio, and minimum ratios for open space, livability space, recreation space and car storage. These are found in Figure B by finding the assigned intensity rating on the scale at the bottom and following its vertical line to intersections with the ratio lines . . .

FHA's LUI system has not met with unalloyed success. It has been a source of confusion to more than one developer; there has been no widespread recognition of the particular appropriateness of the relationships embodied in the LUI scale; and many projects with FHA-insured loans have floundered (although, apparently not for reasons directly related to land-use intensity in most cases). However, architects and planners have considered the LUI standards in planning even non-FHA projects; and it has even been suggested* that this LUI system could be refined and adopted as a standardized measure of land-use intensity.

* *Density: Five Perspectives, a ULI Special Report,* ULI—The Urban Land Institute, Washington, D.C., 1972, p. 59.

Figure B

Land-Use Intensity Scale

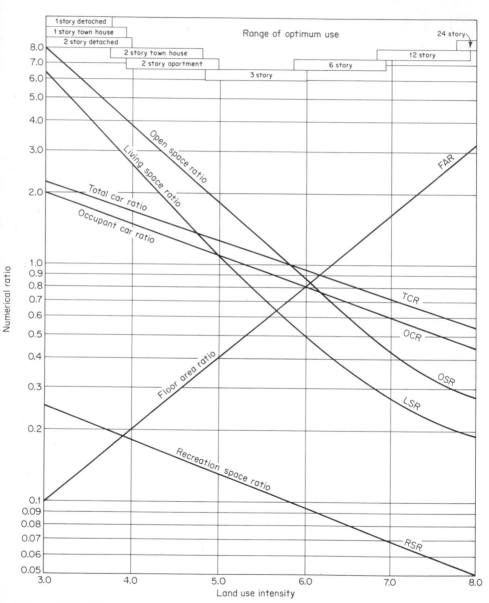

Source: HUD—FHA.

LAND-USE-INTENSITY RATIOS

FAR Floor Area Ratio is maximum square footage of total floor area permitted for each square foot of land area.

OSR Open Space Ratio is minimum square footage of open space required for each square foot of floor area.

LSR Living Space Ratio is minimum square footage of nonvehicular outdoor space required for each square foot of floor area.

RSR Recreation Space Ratio is minimum square footage of recreation space required for each square foot of floor area.

OCR Occupant Car Ratio is minimum number of parking spaces without parking-time limits required for each living unit.

TCR Total Car Ratio is minimum number of parking spaces required for each living unit.

BASIC SCALE

Land-use-intensity number	Floor area ratio
1.0	0.025
2.0	0.050
3.0	0.100
4.0	0.200
5.0	0.400
6.0	0.800
7.0	1.60
8.0	3.20

FAVORABLE LAND-USE-INTENSITY RANGES FOR VARIOUS BUILDING TYPES

Building type	Range of land-use intensity
Single-Family Types	
1-Story Detached	1.0 to 3.8
1-Story Townhouse	2.0 to 3.9
2-Story Detached	2.0 to 4.0
2-Story Townhouse	3.7 to 4.8
Walk-Up Apartments	
2-Story Garden Apartment	3.9 to 5.0
3-Story Apartment	4.9 to 6.0
4-Story Apartment	5.5 to 6.5
Elevator Buildings	
6-Story Apartment	5.9 to 6.9
8-Story Apartment	6.2 to 7.2
10-Story Apartment	6.5 to 7.5
12-Story Apartment	6.8 to 7.9
18-Story Apartment	7.2 to 8.4
24-Story or More	7.7 to 9.4

SINGLE-FAMILY-DWELLING LAND-USE-INTENSITY CRITERIA

Land-use intensity (LUI)	Floor area ratio (FAR)	Open space ratio (OSR)	Livability space ratio (LSR)	Recreation space ratio (RSR)	Occupant car ratio (OCR)	Total car ratio (TCR)
3.0	0.100	0.80	0.65	0.025	2.0	2.2
3.1	0.107	0.80	0.62	0.026	1.9	2.1
3.2	0.115	0.79	0.60	0.026	1.9	2.1
3.3	0.123	0.79	0.58	0.028	1.8	2.0
3.4	0.132	0.78	0.55	0.029	1.7	1.9
3.5	0.141	0.78	0.54	0.030	1.7	1.9
3.6	0.152	0.78	0.53	0.030	1.6	1.8
3.7	0.162	0.77	0.53	0.032	1.6	1.8
3.8	0.174	0.77	0.52	0.033	1.5	1.7
3.9	0.187	0.77	0.52	0.036	1.5	1.7
4.0	0.200	0.76	0.52	0.036	1.4	1.6
4.1	0.214	0.76	0.51	0.039	1.4	1.6
4.2	0.230	0.75	0.51	0.039	1.4	1.5
4.3	0.246	0.75	0.49	0.039	1.3	1.5
4.4	0.264	0.74	0.48	0.042	1.3	1.5
4.5	0.283	0.74	0.48	0.042	1.2	1.4
4.6	0.303	0.73	0.46	0.046	1.2	1.4
4.7	0.325	0.73	0.46	0.046	1.2	1.3
4.8	0.348	0.73	0.45	0.049	1.1	1.3
4.9	0.373	0.72	0.45	0.052	1.1	1.3
5.0	0.400	0.72	0.44	0.052	1.1	1.2
5.1	0.429	0.72	0.43	0.055	1.0	1.2
5.2	0.459	0.72	0.42	0.056	1.0	1.2
5.3	0.492	0.71	0.41	0.059	0.99	1.1
5.4	0.528	0.71	0.41	0.062	0.96	1.1

Source: *Manual of Acceptable Practices*, U.S. Department of Housing and Urban Development, vol. 4, 1973 edition.

WALK-UP-APARTMENT LAND-USE-INTENSITY CRITERIA

Land-use intensity (LUI)	Floor area ratio (FAR)	Open space ratio (OSR)	Livability space ratio (LSR)	Recreation space ratio (RSR)	Occupant car ratio (OCR)	Total car ratio (TCR)
3.6	0.152	0.78	0.53	0.030	1.6	1.8
3.7	0.162	0.77	0.53	0.032	1.6	1.8
3.8	0.174	0.77	0.52	0.033	1.5	1.7
3.9	0.187	0.77	0.52	0.036	1.5	1.7
4.0	0.200	0.76	0.52	0.036	1.4	1.6
4.1	0.214	0.76	0.51	0.039	1.4	1.6
4.2	0.230	0.75	0.51	0.039	1.4	1.6
4.3	0.246	0.75	0.49	0.039	1.3	1.5
4.4	0.264	0.74	0.48	0.042	1.3	1.5
4.5	0.283	0.74	0.48	0.042	1.2	1.4
4.6	0.303	0.73	0.46	0.046	1.2	1.4
4.7	0.325	0.73	0.46	0.046	1.2	1.3
4.8	0.348	0.73	0.45	0.049	1.1	1.3
4.9	0.373	0.72	0.45	0.052	1.1	1.3
5.0	0.400	0.72	0.44	0.052	1.1	1.2
5.1	0.429	0.72	0.43	0.055	1.0	1.2
5.2	0.459	0.72	0.42	0.056	1.0	1.2
5.3	0.492	0.71	0.41	0.059	0.99	1.1
5.4	0.528	0.71	0.41	0.062	0.96	1.1
5.5	0.566	0.71	0.40	0.062	0.93	1.1
5.6	0.606	0.70	0.40	0.065	0.90	1.0
5.7	0.650	0.70	0.40	0.065	0.87	1.0
5.8	0.696	0.69	0.40	0.070	0.84	0.99
5.9	0.746	0.69	0.40	0.075	0.82	0.96
6.0	0.800	0.68	0.40	0.080	0.79	0.93
6.1	0.857	0.68	0.40	0.080	0.77	0.90
6.2	0.919	0.68	0.40	0.083	0.74	0.87
6.3	0.985	0.68	0.40	0.085	0.72	0.85
6.4	1.06	0.68	0.40	0.085	0.70	0.83
6.5	1.13	0.67	0.41	0.090	0.68	0.81

Source: Manual of Acceptable Practices, U.S. Department of Housing and Urban Development, vol. 4, 1973 edition.

HIGH-RISE-APARTMENT LAND-USE-INTENSITY CRITERIA

Land-use intensity (LUI)	Floor area ratio (FAR)	Open space ratio (OSR)	Livability space ratio (LSR)	Recreation space ratio (RSR)	Occupant car ratio (OCR)	Total car ratio (TCR)
5.9	0.746	0.69	0.40	0.075	0.82	0.96
6.0	0.800	0.68	0.40	0.080	0.79	0.93
6.1	0.857	0.68	0.40	0.080	0.77	0.90
6.2	0.919	0.68	0.40	0.083	0.74	0.87
6.3	0.985	0.68	0.40	0.085	0.72	0.85
6.4	1.06	0.68	0.40	0.085	0.70	0.83
6.5	1.13	0.67	0.41	0.090	0.68	0.81
6.6	1.21	0.67	0.41	0.097	0.66	0.79
6.7	1.30	0.67	0.42	0.104	0.64	0.77
6.8	1.39	0.68	0.42	0.104	0.62	0.75
6.9	1.49	0.68	0.43	0.104	0.60	0.73
7.0	1.60	0.68	0.43	0.112	0.58	0.71
7.1	1.72	0.68	0.45	0.115	0.57	0.69
7.2	1.84	0.69	0.46	0.115	0.56	0.67
7.3	1.97	0.70	0.47	0.118	0.54	0.65
7.4	2.11	0.71	0.49	0.127	0.52	0.63
7.5	2.26	0.72	0.50	0.136	0.50	0.61
7.6	2.42	0.75	0.51	0.145	0.49	0.60
7.7	2.60	0.76	0.52	0.145	0.47	0.58
7.8	2.79	0.81	0.56	0.145	0.46	0.56
7.9	2.99	0.83	0.57	0.150	0.45	0.55
8.0	3.20	0.86	0.61	0.160	0.44	0.54

Source: *Manual of Acceptable Practices*, U.S. Department of Housing and Urban Development, vol. 4, 1973 edition.

9 How long to hold land

A rough guide for land speculators: Land that doesn't produce income during the holding period should have the prospect of doubling in price in five years.

Mr. A. just sold a piece of land for three times what he paid for it ten years ago. Fantastic return, right? Well, actually, Mr. A's return was equal to less than 12 percent compound interest—not counting the deductions for real estate taxes, a sales commission, and title and transfer costs. Not necessarily a disappointing return, but hardly fantastic.

This example illustrates a point: If one is to invest in vacant land not producing income during the holding period, a very large price increase may be necessary to produce even a normal return. At times of high yields on other investments, it is not unusual for seasoned buyers and sellers of vacant land to require 12 percent to 15 percent returns. To provide such a return on an investment (unleveraged), land has to double in value in five years or so—assuming no expenses of holding the land or selling it off.

If land is to be held longer than five years, the rate of appreciation each year must become substantially larger than it was in early years to provide the same return. In Case 1, 25 percent appreciation was needed in the sixth year to provide the same return that only 16 percent provided in the first year.

Of course, favorable terms (leverage) can help, but the longer the land is held, the less the terms enhance the yield. (See Case 2.) In choosing between tracts, investors often must weigh more favorable terms for one tract against the better appreciation potential of another.

Too many people feel that buying vacant land near a growing city is a sure way of making a big return. After all, nearly everyone knows of at least one parcel that sold back then for such-and-such and is now worth many times such-and-such. However, not everyone is as quick to remember that (1) without hindsight, many people bought other parcels which didn't appreciate so much, and that (2) even huge appreciation *over a long period of time* may be equal to only a modest return. To be sure, there *are* opportunities for substantial returns in buying and selling vacant tracts, but adequate returns are not *assured.* In this complicated field, timing is critical, and there is no substitute for sound judgment.

CASE 1

Mr. B., a land speculator, considers buying a 10-acre wooded tract. He sizes up the situation like this:

1. Minimum purchase price of $10,000, all in cash. (Seller needs cash. Mr. B. doubts if mortgage loan available on this security.)

2. No income potential during holding period.

3. Real estate taxes and other minor expenses likely to approximate $200 per year.

4. Will be able to sell tract himself, presumably for cash. Anticipates 2 percent or so of sale price for title and transfer costs.

5. Needs minimum return of 12 percent per year (true rate, compounded annually, before income taxes) to make this attractive relative to other investment opportunities.

Question: How soon would this parcel have to double in price?
  Answer: Between five and six years.
            If it took six years or longer for the sale price to double, Mr. B.'s return would be too low. Note also how the overall rate of appreciation needed each year rises rather quickly.

Investment year	Cash outlays and allowance for minimum return on investment (Purchase price—$10,000)		Minimum sale price needed at end of this year	Rate of appreciation needed this year
1st	12% return 1,200 Expenses 200		($11,400 ÷ 98%) $11,633	16%
2nd	12% return 1,368 Expenses 200		($12,968 ÷ 98%) $13,233	16%
3rd	12% return 1,556 Expenses 200		($14,724 ÷ 98%) $15,024	18%
4th	12% return 1,767 Expenses 200		($16,691 ÷ 98%) $17,032	20%
5th	12% return 2,003 Expenses 200		($18,894 ÷ 98%) $19,280	22%
6th	12% return 2,267 Expenses 200		($21,361 ÷ 98%) $21,797	25%

CASE 2

Another speculator, Mr. C., buys a vacant tract. His projection:

1. $100,000 purchase price. $25,000 down. Balance of $75,000 on contract with 9% interest. Interest only in first year. Then, one payment of $75,000 plus accrued interest at end of each year for the next ten years. Prepayment permitted after four years.

2. All cash sale six years after purchase. Allowance for sales commission and transfer costs at 10 percent of sale price.

3. Minor income, sufficient to meet expenses.

4. Hoped-for return of 15 percent per year (a simple interest return only on amounts paid out).

Question: If price doubles over his six-year holding period, will Mr. C. get his hoped-for return?

Answer: Almost.

	Cash outlays	Hoped-for return on cash outlays		
Immediate	$ 25,000 (D.P.)	6 years @ $25,000 × 0.15		$22,500
End of 1st year	6,750 (Int.)	5 years @ 6,750 × 0.15		5,062
End of 2nd year	6,750 (Int.)	4 years @ 6,750 × 0.15		4,050
	7,500 (Prin.)	4 years @ 7,500 × 0.15		4,500
End of 3rd year	6,075 (Int.)	3 years @ 6,075 × 0.15		2,734
	7,500 (Prin.)	3 years @ 7,500 × 0.15		3,375
End of 4th year	5,400 (Int.)	2 years @ 5,400 × 0.15		1,620
	7,500 (Prin.)	2 years @ 7,500 × 0.15		2,250
End of 5th year	4,725 (Int.)	1 year @ 4,725 × 0.15		709
	7,500 (Prin.)	1 year @ 7,500 × 0.15		1,125
End of 6th year	4,050 (Int.)			
	45,000 (Prin.)			
	20,000 (10%)			
	$153,750			$47,925

Hoped-for sale price at end of six years $201,675

10 Ideal maximum distances to daily activities

In selecting land for a residential development, one may be guided by the following illustration which suggests maximum distances home buyers may be willing to travel to certain facilities.

Any guidelines of this sort are necessarily a bit arbitrary, but these are considered useful. These distances are considered *ideal* (or safe) maximums for most urban areas, but they can be knowledgeably exceeded in special cases. For example, if busing to the grade school is generally acceptable in a market area, the distance may be stretched somewhat.

Remember that travel time and convience are usually more important than distance. Remember also that attitudes will vary somewhat because of differences in income levels and other factors.

IDEAL MAXIMUM DISTANCES
TO DAILY ACTIVITIES

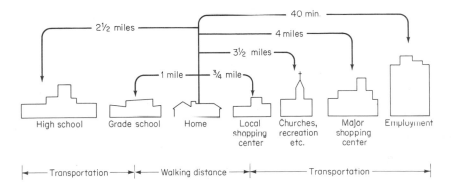

Ideal maximum distances to daily activities

From: *The Community Builders Handbook,* reprinted with permission of ULI—the Urban Land Institute, 1200 18th Street, N.W., Washington, D.C. 20036.

The Walk-Away Test

The Walk-Away Test: Here is a very simple way to assess the noise levels at a residential site.

Today, just about everybody knows that noise pollution can be a problem.

Yet most tracts for residential development are purchased, appraised, and financed without any *objective* tests of the noise levels. One reason for this is that some of these tests are fairly sophisticated and require special equipment and knowledge.

Well, the Walk-Away Test is quick and easy. Here is how the Department of Housing and Urban Development describes it.

> The Walk-Away Test requires two men who exchange roles as speaker and listener; thus, each person should have normal hearing and an average voice. To perform the test, you will need a 100-ft. tape measure and some reading material with which both persons are unfamiliar.

> The speaker should stand at fixed location, while the listener, starting at a distance of 2 or 3 ft., backs slowly away. The speaker should hold the reading material at chest height in such a way as not to block the direct path from himself to the listener. He should not raise his voice in an attempt to maintain communication.

> At some point the listener will find that he can understand only a scattered word or two over a period of 10 seconds or more. At this point, measure the distance between the listener and the speaker.

> For consistent and accurate results, this procedure should be repeated several times during each visit and the distances should be averaged. Also, the roles of speaker and listener should be reversed to average out variations of normal speaking levels and hearing acuity. After each visit, evaluate the site's overall noise levels by using [the accompanying table].*

Since noise levels will usually vary from hour to hour and from day to day, this test should be performed when noise is apt to be worst (for example, when a train or plane is passing or during peak auto traffic) and when noise is apt to be most annoying (for example, between 10:00 P.M. and midnight, when people are trying to go to sleep). Also, the stationary person on the test team—the speaker—should stand on the tract he is testing at the homesite nearest the worst source of noise.

If, at any time during the test, the noise level is found to be unacceptable, one must then consider whether the location of the dwellings on the parcel can be changed,

---

* Theodore J. Schultz and Nancy M. McMahon, *Noise Assessment Guidelines,* U.S. Department of Housing and Urban Development, BBN Report No. 2176.

whether the noise can be blocked out effectively, or whether the parcel should be rejected.

Consider an example:

>An appraiser and his assistant want to test the noise levels on a particular tract being considered for a residential development. They make three brief visits to the parcel on weekdays. On their first visit (between 8:00 A.M. and 9:00 A.M.—during heavy going-to-work traffic), the distances where understanding just becomes difficult (48 feet, 53 feet, 51 feet, and 52 feet) average 51 feet. On their second visit (between 4:00 P.M. and 5:00 P.M.—a time of heavy going-home traffic), the distances average 55 feet. On their third visit (between 10:00 P.M. and 11:00 P.M.—a time when many are trying to go to sleep), their measurements averaged 74 feet.

>They check with the table and rate the noise level on this parcel "Normally Acceptable."

This is not the only test of noise levels. It may not be the best. But it clearly beats the usual procedure: no objective test at all.

SITE EXPOSURE TO
OVERALL NOISE LEVELS

Distance where understanding becomes very difficult	*Acceptability category*
More than 70 feet	Clearly Acceptable (The noise exposure is such that both the indoor and outdoor environments are pleasant.)
26–70 feet	Normally Acceptable (The noise exposure is great enough to be of some concern, but common building constructions will make the indoor environment acceptable, even for sleeping quarters, and the outdoor environment will be reasonably pleasant for recreation and play.)
7–25 feet	Normally Unacceptable (The noise exposure is significantly more severe so that unusual and costly building constructions are necessary to ensure some tranquillity indoors, and barriers must be erected between the site and prominent noise sources to make the outdoor environment tolerable.)
Less than 7 feet	Clearly Unacceptable (The noise exposure at the site is so severe that the construction costs to make the indoor environment acceptable would be prohibitive and the outdoor environment would still be intolerable.)

Nine rules of thumb for off-street parking

How much off-street parking should be provided?

Here are some of the more popular rules of thumb:

1. **At least two spaces for each detached dwelling, condominium unit, or cooperative unit.**

2. **At least 1.5 spaces for each dwelling unit in a rental project.**

3. **One space for every 500 to 1,000 square feet of general office space in a central location.**

4. **One space for each 250 square feet of general office space in a suburban location.**

5. **One space for each 150 square feet of medical office space.**

6. **One space per guest room plus one space for every two to three restaurant seats in a motor hotel—restaurant development.**

7. **One space for every three to five seat spaces in a church.**

8. **Five to ten spaces for every lane in a bowling center.**

9. **Parking lots (including access drives and landscaped areas) in ratios of open space to building floor areas of 3 to 1 in shopping centers and 4 to 1 or 5 to 1 for freestanding stores.**

Some of these can be useful for sizing up parking needs in a preliminary way, but every one of these rules of thumb must be qualified in several ways.

In deciding if one or more of these rules of thumb may be useful to you, here are some important considerations:

· In some cases, the intelligent goal is this: Provide parking to the extent that it is likely to be used *regularly* if you can afford to do so. Usually, it does not pay to provide parking that will be used only rarely.

· Competition and custom have something to do with how much parking is provided. For example, one of the factors to be considered in planning a major office building is how much parking is offered in competitive buildings.

· Obviously, zoning requirements are an important influence.

· So are the availability and use of public transit and other means of transportation. To the extent that people are likely to arrive at a facility by public
transit, via taxis, or on foot, the need for parking spaces is diminished. Parking requirements of downtown office buildings and stores are often a fraction of those in suburban office buildings and stores.

· Parking demand may vary from one price range to another. For example,
tenants in prestige apartments may have both more autos and more visitors
than those in modest apartments.

· Even the age level of tenants can make a difference. For example, parking requirements may be less for dwelling units designed to house persons of ad-
vanced age.

· Some types of offices need higher parking indexes than others. There can be
very wide variations in employee density and in the number of visitors from
one type of office to another. In the case of medical offices, parking is often
planned in terms of so many spaces per doctor.

· The same thing is generally true about variations from one type of store to
another. For example, a supermarket normally needs a higher parking
index than a furniture store.

· Other things being equal, stores and offices in shopping centers can usually
function well with lower parking indexes than individual stores and office
buildings. This appears to be partly because shopping-center patrons may
stop at several stores in one visit, and partly because peak hours are usually
not the same for all of the tenants in a shopping center.

· The appropriate parking index may vary with the size of a project. For
example, often there is an inverse relationship between the size of the
church building and the size of its parking lot. (Probably, this is partly due to
central locations, higher unit land values, and/or use of public transit
associated with some larger churches.)

A parking index (Example: One parking space for each 250 square feet of office
space) is usually to be preferred over a parking ratio (Example: 1.5 square feet of
parking area to each square foot of office space). This is true even if both lead to
parking lots of the same size. Why? It's useful to keep in mind that the goal is to
provide the most appropriate number of parking spaces—and the amount of
parking area required to do this can change over time, as we shall see in the next
chapter.

13 400 square feet per parking space

A widely used guideline: For preliminary planning of sizable parking lots, allow 400 square feet of land for each parking space.

In the mid-1970s, there were indications that this might be reduced in some cases.

For years, architects, developers, planners, and others have used this popular guideline for *preliminary* planning. It allows for drives, for limited landscaped areas, and for small areas that cannot be used efficiently.

It will be obvious to the reader that some parcels of land permit more efficient parking layouts than others because of differences in size, shape, access, and topography.

Further, the size of parking spaces may be intelligently varied for different conditions. Narrow parking spaces may be appropriate for all-day parking on costly land, while spaces of more generous size may be appropriate in a suburban retail facility where land costs are relatively low and parking turnover is relatively high.

In the 1970s, the trend toward smaller autos—the so-called mid-size, compact, and subcompact cars—justified a smaller average area per parking space in some cases. Obviously, a less-than-14-foot-long Gremlin doesn't need a parking space as large as an over-19-foot-long Oldsmobile; and by 1975, a majority of the cars using many parking lots were small cars. If, instead of laying out all of the spaces in a large parking lot for full-size cars (say, at 9 by 19 feet), a planner lays out half or more for smaller cars (say, at 7.5 by 15 feet), the total land area required can be reduced by as much as one-third.

14 ULI's parking index

How much parking should be provided in a suburban shopping center? Here is a good guide: 5.5 parking spaces for every 1,000 square feet of gross leasable store area.

This standard has been well supported, but it can be intelligently varied in some individual cases.

Here is a success story.

For a long time, people who had something to say about shopping-center design—developers, lenders, chain-store tenants, architects, zoning officials, and planners—thought in terms of parking ratios: so many square feet of open space (parking, drives, landscaping) for each square foot of building area. The most common ratio required was 3 square feet for each square foot of building.

Well, a lot of shopping-center professionals noticed that a sizable percentage of their parking spaces were vacant most of the time. They felt that their parking lots might be too generous in size, and they sought more information on parking needs. They got it in the form of an authoritative study* issued by the Urban Land Institute. Based upon a valid sampling† of 270 shopping centers, ULI came to these eye-opening conclusions:

1. If virtually all of the patrons came to a shopping center by auto, 5.5 parking spaces for each 1,000 square feet of gross *leasable* store area will normally be adequate.

   This parking index was found to meet parking requirements in all but the ten peak shopping hours each year.

   This recommended standard includes parking for employees and a margin to enable free traffic movement. It applies fairly consistently to centers of all sizes.

2. To the extent that the shoppers arrive by public transit and on foot, this parking index can be reduced. Shopping centers (or districts) in central locations with much walk-in business and public transit service may need just a fraction of this parking capacity.

---

* *Parking Requirements for Shopping Centers* (Technical Bulletin 53, a Research Project sponsored by the Research Foundation of the International Council of Shopping Centers and conducted by the Urban Land Institute). Permission to discuss conclusions of this study was given by ULI—the Urban Land Institute, 1200 Eighteenth Street, NW, Washington, D.C. 20036.

† Deliberately selected so as to be fairly representative.

3. Office space in a center may not necessitate additional parking; typically, adding office space up to 20 percent of gross leasable store areas results in no noticeable increase in peak parking demand. This is because peak hours tend to be different for offices than for stores.

ULI's index was selected because it will typically meet customers' parking needs in over 99.5 percent of the shopping hours each year. To provide additional parking spaces that would be empty over 99.5 percent of the time would be wasteful.

How does ULI's recommended parking standard compare with the old 3 square feet to 1 square foot parking standard? Well, in many cases, following the old standard would result in over one-third more parking spaces than ULI's standard—spaces likely to be used rarely or never.

This is an excellent example of how research can lead to better guidelines for planning.

Adjustments to ULI's recommended parking index can—and should—be made in some specific cases. An uncommon tenant mix could make a difference. (For example, furniture stores often have less traffic per square foot of leasable area than drugstores.) Physical barriers might limit a trading area (and thus the customer potential) somewhat. In the case of an existing center that is to be expanded, data on parking patterns in the past might suggest some modification in the parking index.

Hourly Parking Requirements

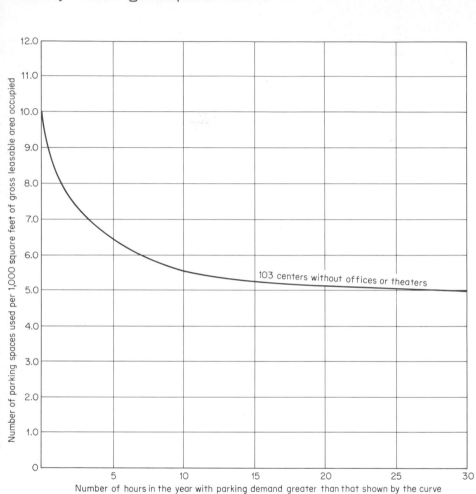

Source: Parking Requirements for Shopping Centers. Reprinted with permission of ULI—the Urban Land Institute, 1200 18th Street, N.W., Washington, D.C. 20036.

This chart shows the use of parking spaces in 103 shopping centers without office space or theaters. Note that customer parking demand exceeded ULI recommended standard (5.5 spaces per 1,000 square feet) in only ten shopping hours a year—less than one-half of 1 percent of the total shopping hours.

 When to build a parking garage

When can you afford to build a parking garage?

One popular answer: When land values have risen to the point that the cost of surface parking (per stall) exceeds the cost of multilevel parking (per stall).

This is too simplistic.

Of course, relative cost is a big factor. One of the biggest. But there are others:

1. A building can be depreciated, thus providing tax shelter. Land cannot.

2. Sites and improvements are often assessed at substantially different levels relative to their market values. And remember that the real estate tax burden is often the largest single item of expense for income properties.

3. Multilevel parking can provide some very welcome protection from extreme weather.

4. Some drivers have an aversion to multilevel parking.

5. In some cases, contiguous land just may not be available to provide additional surface parking.

6. It is often important to have parking stalls located within convenient walking distances of stores, offices, or apartments. In some large developments, this may not be possible with surface parking alone.

7. Maintenance costs vary.

Basically, this proposition is a sound one, but the wise real estate professional would not rely on it alone and ignore these other factors which can be vitally important.

16 How many people are needed to support various types of developments

Several rules of thumb suggest how many people may be needed to support various types of developments. Examples:

1. **About 25,000 people for each regulation 18-hole golf course.**

2. **About 1,500 to 2,000 people for each bowling lane.**

3. **About 30,000 people for each tunnel-type car wash with gas pumps.**

4. **For shopping centers: from about 2,000 families for a less-than-100,000-square-foot (gross store area) neighborhood center to something on the order of 100,000 families for a million-square-foot regional center.**

There is no mystery about the popularity of rules like these. They are easy to apply. They are interesting. And some have considerable merit—as rough preliminary checks.

However, some limitations and cautions are fairly obvious too. People may live (or work or play) near a facility but not be potential customers of that facility at all. A car-wash operator cannot count on people who don't have autos. A yacht dealer cannot count on people with modest incomes. Wealthy owners of detached dwellings are much less likely to patronize coin laundries than middle-income apartment dwellers.

Looking at the *number* of people in a trading area is looking at just one of the four "people factors" in feasibility work:

1. How many people are there (will there be)?

2. How much money do (will) they have to spend?

3. What do (will) they spend it for?

4. Where do (will) they spend it?

Not surprisingly, rules of thumb and guidelines are also used to help project:

1. How much money people have to spend. (Example: Home values and apartment rentals in a trading area can be translated into rough estimates of family incomes, as shown in Part III.)

2. What they spend the money for. (Examples: Middle-income families typically spend about 10 percent of their incomes on primary shoppers' goods found in department stores, clothing stores, shoe stores, and furniture stores. Generally, the higher the income level, the smaller the percentage of income spent on such necessities as food and shelter.)

3. Where they spend the money. (Example: A neighborhood shopping center usually draws most of its *regular* patronage from one to two miles away, while a regional center may draw customers from six to eight miles away on a continuing basis.*)

---

* Travel time and convenience of access are usually more telling than the distance. Most of the methods, guidelines, and formulas devised to help decide where shoppers are likely to make their major retail purchases recognize travel time (or distance) and the size of the shopping facility as the two most important factors. (Several of these are updates and refinements of work by William J. Reilly which was first published in 1929 and often referred to as Reilly's Law or the Law of Retail Gravitation.) However, other factors can also influence shoppers. (Does the facility have a climate-controlled mall? Is parking ample and free of charge? What are the reputations of the stores? Is there an important difference in prices?)

Part II

Lot Sizes
and Shapes

So far as we can see with any certainty, the quality of value has longer and more constantly attached to the ownership of land than to any other valuable thing.
—HENRY GEORGE

17 Hoffman Rule

Hoffman Rule: The front half of a 100-foot-deep lot is worth two-thirds of that lot's value.

Though more than 100 years old, this depth rule is still being used—directly or indirectly—by many today.

This "rule" is credited to Judge Murray Hoffman in 1866. It is believed to be the first generally recognized depth rule.

The basic idea behind depth rules (and the tables of depth factors based on them) is a simple one. In any particular neighborhood in which lot frontage is much more important than lot depth, one may:

a. identify a standard lot depth, . . .*

b. note that, other things being equal, deeper lots are worth more than shallower lots, . . .

c. recognize that the front part of a lot is worth more than the rear part, and . . .

d. try to say how much lot value is increased or decreased by variations from the standard depth.

Numerous tables of depth factors—most of them based upon the Hoffman Rule and the 4-3-2-1 Rule † —have been formulated, and they are in use by thousands of real estate tax assessors and by others in the real estate field.

The Hoffman Rule was made up in a horse-and-buggy era. (The first American gasoline-powered automobile was built by the Duryea brothers more than a quarter of a century later.) Now this country is more than twice as old as it was then, and life is very different. Yet depth tables based on the Hoffman Rule are still in wide use—mostly by people who never heard of Judge Murray Hoffman and his 1866 rule.

Some of the questions surrounding the use of this rule are set out in the next chapter.

* Frequently but improperly taken to be 100 feet, perhaps because Judge Hoffman started out on that basis.

† See Chapter 19.

55

Hoffman-Neill Rule

Hoffman-Neill Rule: Elaborating on the Hoffman Rule, journalist Henry H. Neill published a table of depth factors set out on the next page.

Reliance on this table is questionable.

Even if you are not suspicious of factors devised in another century, there are some bothersome questions here. Even if you aren't concerned by mathematical aberrations in the table, there are still questions. Consider just a few of them:

1. What proof has ever been offered to support these particular figures?

2. How could you justify going into various neighborhoods—young, old, modest, prestigious, city, suburban—and always starting out with the assumption that the standard lot depth for the neighborhood is 100 feet?

3. Does the amount of frontage make no difference? (Does a 100- by 120-foot lot necessarily have the same per-front-foot value as a neighboring 20- by 120-foot lot?)

4. How can you ignore differences in size that may affect the highest and best use? (A 100- by 150-foot lot will normally have a quite different highest and best use than a neighboring 100- by 10-foot lot—and usefulness is the prime determinant of value.)

One can raise these, or very similar, questions about the validity of other depth tables as well, as the reader will see in the next two chapters.

DEPTH FACTORS

Depth	Percent of front foot value of 100-foot lot	Depth	Percent of front foot value of 100-foot lot
5 ft.	17.0%	110 ft.	106.0%
10	26.0	120	111.7
15	33.0	130	116.9
20	39.0	140	122.3
25	44.0	150	127.3
30	49.0	160	132.1
35	54.0	170	137.0
40	58.0	180	141.5
45	62.0	190	146.0
50	66.0	200	150.0
55	70.7	220	159.0
60	74.4	240	167.5
65	77.9	260	175.3
70	81.5	280	183.0
75	84.8	300	191.0
80	88.0	320	198.3
85	91.3	340	205.5
90	94.3	360	212.3
95	97.3	380	219.0
100	100.0	400	225.0

Example of Use: A real estate tax assessor wants to know the value of a certain 100- by 300-foot lot. He finds that 100-foot-deep lots in the same neighborhood are selling for $200 per front foot. Using the 300-foot depth factor from the Hoffman-Neill table above, he values this 100- by 300-foot lot at (100 front feet @ $200 × 1.910) $38,200.

The 4-3-2-1 Rule

The 4-3-2-1 Rule: In a lot of standard depth, this rule gives . . .

	SECOND STREET
40% of the lot's value to the front 25%, .	**40%**
30% of value to the next 25%, . . .	**30%**
20% of value to the next 25%, . . .	**20%**
and 10% of value to the rear 25%.	**10%**

Though this old depth rule is of doubtful reliability, it is very widely used.

Here we are looking at another horse-and-buggy depth rule which has survived for decades.

This depth rule is often used for commercial and residential lots in locations where frontage is much more important than depth. It is not commonly used for large tracts.

It is not hard to see several reasons for the popularity of the 4-3-2-1 Rule:

1. Real estate appraisers and assessors often have to deal with problems that can be "solved" by use of a depth rule.

2. The pseudoscientific sound of this rule is, in itself, impressive to some people.

3. With some types of lots in some locations, one can see that the *general* pattern is like this.

However, the informed real estate professional will want to recognize these cautions and limitations:

1. While the general pattern is often like this, and no research can be cited to refute the 4-3-2-1 Rule, neither can one cite persuasive research to show that this depth rule is more reliable than any of a dozen others.*

---

* Regression analysis, rarely applied to real estate problems prior to the 1970s, is now increasingly used to analyze market data. Expertly applied to data in many submarkets, regression analysis could provide convincing support for or refutation of such depth rules as *general* propositions.

EXAMPLE OF APPLICATION OF 4-3-2-1 RULE

The standard lot in the neighborhood is 60 by 120 feet and sells for $6,000. According to the 4-3-2-1 Rule, this value may be allocated:

Front 30 ft. of depth	$2,400 (40%)
Next 30 ft. of depth	1,800 (30%)
Next 30 ft. of depth	1,200 (20%)
Rear 30 ft. of depth	600 (10%)
Full 120 ft. of depth	$6,000 (100%)

Knowing this, one might feel that an (unusually shallow) 50- by 60-ft. lot here is worth (70% of $6,000) $4,200.

2. It is difficult or impossible to apply this rule in a consistent manner.

   Many who use the 4-3-2-1 Rule reluctantly adopt the assumption that all parts of any quarter of a lot are equal: a square foot at the rear of the front quarter is worth just as much as a square foot at the front. This assumption contradicts the very basis of this rule—that unit values decline as one moves back from the frontage.

   However, if one doesn't make this assumption, how are various units "graded" within each quarter? If the 4-3-2-1 Rule is used within each quarter, then a square foot at the rear of the first quarter would be valued higher than a square foot at the front of the second quarter, and that wouldn't do at all.

3. If one is to use this rule in a specific case, one must first know the "standard depth." Just what is the standard depth? Some take it to be the typical platted lot depth in the neighborhood. Others see it as the typical lot depth in use. Some advance good arguments to support the position that the optimum economic depth by today's standards should be taken as the standard depth. It can be very difficult to pin down the standard depth precisely—that is, to the exclusion of somewhat varying figures—in some neighborhoods.

4. A difference in lot depth can mean a difference in highest and best use. If by local ordinance, the minimum lot size on which one may erect a dwelling is 4,500 square feet, a 50- by 75-foot lot (3,750 square feet and nonbuildable) may be worth much less than 90 percent of what the standard 50- by 100-foot lot (5,000 square feet and buildable) is worth. Changing the depth (and the area and shape) of a commercial lot can change its use potential drastically too. Just applying the 4-3-2-1 Rule—or any other depth rule—in such cases can lead to ridiculous results.

Despite all this, the 4-3-2-1 Rule is still accepted as something of a standard in the real estate field by many appraisers and assessors. It shows the incredible staying power of some old rules of thumb in the face of radical changes in real estate markets.

20

The parabolic formula

Substituting this formula for the popular 4-3-2-1 Rule has some mechanical advantages:

(Depth factor)^2 = 2 (Depth of lot) (Constant for lot of known value)

Decades ago, real estate professionals recognized that the formula for a parabola* might be used in lieu of the 4-3-2-1 Rule. Values assigned to different depths are roughly similar:

Street		Street	
40%		50.0%	
30%		20.7%	
20%		15.9%	
10%		13.4%	
4-3-2-1 Rule		This Formula	

The advantage of using this formula is that one can apply it to all lot depths with mathematical consistency—something not possible with the 4-3-2-1 Rule.

One may derive a depth factor for the front 67 percent of a lot. One may allocate part of the value of a 324-foot-deep lot to the rear 87 feet. All on a (mathematically) consistent basis.

Consider an example:

> Suppose you want to value lots along First Street. A 50-by 150-foot lot just sold for $200 per front foot. Then 150 feet is the depth of the lot of known value, and the constant (or base or par or 100 percent or 1.00) for this depth factor would be 0.00333. †

---

* A particular curve recognized in plane geometry.

† The formula: (Depth factor)² = 2 (Depth of lot) (Constant for lot of known value)

By substitution: (1.00)² = 2 (150)   (Constant)
                          1   =   300   × Constant
                    0.00333   =   Constant

Now you are ready to relate this base (or comparable) lot to any lot of comparable location. Say you want to relate this sale to a 50- by 300-foot lot nearby. Using this formula, your value estimate is (50 front feet @ $200 × depth factor 1.415*) $14,150.

Yes, use of this formula will cure one problem of the 4-3-2-1 Rule; you can apply it with mechanical consistency to all depths. But what about all the other questions raised in the preceding chapter? If the assumptions implicit in this method don't "square" with what's happening in the submarket you're working in, you can be awfully wrong—*with mechanical consistency.*

---

* The formula: (Depth factor)² = 2 (Depth of lot) (Constant for lot of known value)

By substitution: (Depth factor)² = 2 (300) (0.00333)
(Depth factor)² = 1.998
Depth factor = $\sqrt{1.998}$
Depth factor = 1.415

 Other depth rules

There are several other depth rules and depth tables. Every one should be viewed skeptically.

Today, a wide variety of depth tables are in use. Some assume a standard depth of 100 feet, and some are computed for other "standard" lot depths. Some give a factor for every foot of depth from 1 to 400 feet or more.* Most of these tables give adjustment factors which the user multiplies times a front-foot value to adjust for depth. However, some tables actually offer dollars-and-cents "values" per front foot or per square foot for various depths.

Most of these tables are simply adaptations of the two "granddaddies" of depth rules: the 1866 Hoffman Rule and the old 4-3-2-1 Rule. For general use, not one is free of serious doubts raised in the last four chapters.

Most assessors across the country use such tables regularly. Given their operating budgets and other constraints and millions of lots to value, resorting to some admittedly arbitrary guidelines may be absolutely necessary if these lots are to be valued on a consistent basis—and, let's tell the truth: in the real estate tax assessment field, it can sometimes be more important to be consistent (in terms of procedure) than it is to be right (in terms of market value).

However, highly qualified professionals know that no depth rule or table is a panacea. They know that the *general* premise is sound; with many groups of lots, front portions do indeed contribute more to value than rear portions, but they want to know *how much* more. The authoritative answer to this question is found only in market data, not in some precomputed table.

If examination of data in a particular submarket supports the assumptions which are implicit in a particular depth rule, formula, or table, then the appraiser has a good tool for use in that submarket. To use such a tool without convincing support for it would be to let a questionable device take the place of informed judgment.

---

* While one may argue that this is necessary for real estate tax assessment purposes, it can be artificial in the extreme. Among lots prized much more for frontage than for depth, a 100- by 396-foot lot would theoretically be preferred over a 100- by 395-foot lot (other things being equal); but one setting out to measure the value of such a minute difference in the market might make Don Quixote seem, by comparison, a pragmatist.

22 Rules for irregular lots

There are rules for valuing triangular lots and other unusual lots which are even more questionable.

So far in Part II, all of the rules have been for rectangular lots. Since assessors and others often have to deal with nonrectangular lots, it is useful to take at least a brief look at some of the tables and rules developed for them.

The example on the next page is reasonably representative of many tables which purport to give value figures for triangular lots. Clearly, reliance solely on such tables could lead to ridiculous valuations in some cases. For very shallow lots, such tables often suggest that a triangular lot with extensive frontage (i.e., with its base along the street) is not a great deal more valuable than a zero-frontage lot (i.e., triangular lot with its apex at the street) of the same dimensions.

For example, would you be willing to assume that Lot A with its extensive street frontage is necessarily worth only about 38 percent more than Lot B, which has no street frontage at all?

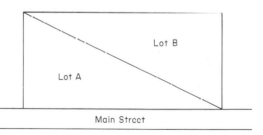

Or, would you feel confident in assuming that triangular Lot C necessarily has essentially the same highest and best use as a rectangular lot twice its size?

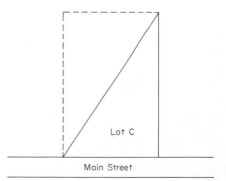

If you could accept that, would
you be willing to believe that
there couldn't be a radical difference in highest and best use
between triangular Lot D, which
has no street frontage, and a rectangular lot twice its size with extensive street frontage?

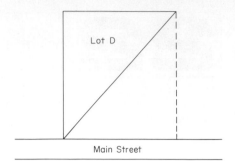

An essential point is this, isn't it: A table that tries to relate values of two sites that
may well have markedly different use potentials is a table that can lead the unin-
formed or lazy person to appallingly bad conclusions.

Rules devised for valuing triangular lots include the 60-40 Rule (use 60 percent of
the value of a rectangular lot of the same depth if the base of the triangle is along
the street, 40 percent if the apex of the triangle is at the street), the 65-35 Rule,
and the 75-25 Rule. In any particular case, at least two of the three are unreliable.
By the time one finds out which, if indeed any, is applicable, who needs the rule?

There are rules for dealing with so-called flatiron parcels (sites with streets on
two sides), four-sided figures with no two sides parallel, through lots, and other
lots of unusual shapes and frontages.

Not one of these methods or rules or tables can be accepted without question.
Not one can be dependably substituted in a specific case for the individual analysis needed to answer these questions:

1. What is the site's highest and best use?

2. What can we learn from individual comparisons with comparable sites in
   the same submarket?

3. If the site has income potential, how does that income potential relate to
   its market value.

TABLE FOR VALUING TRIANGULAR LOTS

Lot depth (along perpendicular)	Percent of full (rectangular lot) value with base of triangle along street	Percent of full (rectangular lot) value with apex of triangle at street
10 ft.	54%	46%
20	56	44
30	58	42
40	59	41
50	61	39
60	62	38
70	63	37
80	64	36
90	65	35
100	66	34
110	67	33
120	68	32
130	69	31
140	70	30
150	71	29
200	75	25

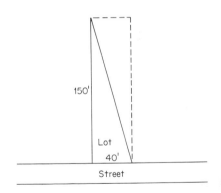

Use: To value a triangular lot with one street frontage:

    a. Extend that triangle into a rectangle.

    b. Value the resultant rectangular lot as usual.

    c. Multiply that value by percentage indicated in table.

Example: *a.* Extend to 40- by 150-foot rectangle.

    b. Value rectangular lot as usual. (Say 40 feet @ $250 = $10,000)

    c. Apply percentage from table. (71% of $10,000 = $7,100)

(Cont.)

TABLE FOR VALUING TRIANGULAR LOTS

(Cont.)

Note: If lot to be valued is irregular triangle (with no right angles), one can:

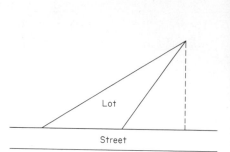

a. First, extend lot to right triangle (as at right)

b. then proceed with steps as outlined above, and

c. finally, subtract part of value estimate imputable to the added portion of right triangle (which is itself a smaller right triangle).

 **Rules for corner lots**

Corner locations can enhance site values. Is there an easy way to find out how much?

There are a flock of corner-influence tables to choose from, but one should not place primary reliance upon them.

In a retail area, a corner lot can be worth twice as much as an inside lot of the same size—or even more. Usually, the highest unit values one finds in a community "attach" to corner locations.

Why are corner lots often prized far more highly than inside lots nearby? Frequent answers: greater visibility to motorists and pedestrians, more light and air, better ingress and egress, and greater flexibility of use.

In specific cases, it is not enough to know that lot value is enhanced by a corner location (over the value of an otherwise comparable *inside* lot); one often needs to know how *much* it is enhanced. Corner-influence tables—very simply—are attempts to provide the answer.

The amount of enhancement depends upon several factors. What is the highest and best use of the lot? Is corner influence considered very advantageous for this use in this particular submarket? Relative to the main street, how attractive is the side street? What about traffic (auto and foot) patterns here? Are use restrictions for corner lots different from those for inside lots? Is the corner influence acting over a small area (or frontage) or a large area (or frontage)?

On page 69 is an example of one type of corner-influence table which has been widely used. When you see a table very similar to this, there's a good chance that it was derived directly or indirectly from work done by W. A. Somers and others *before the turn of the century.*

As in this example, many (perhaps most) corner-influence tables in wide use today assume that corner influence does not extend beyond 100 feet along either the main street or the side street. Typically, one who uses such a table simply values any additional frontage (i.e., any frontage in excess of 100 feet along either street) separately at the front foot rate applicable to *inside* lots.

The table on page 70 has a different format and different factors, but its aim and some of its assumptions are the same. Percentages set out in this example are generally consistent with the widely recognized Zangerle Curve.*

* If one follows guidelines developed decades ago by John J. Zangerle, one might estimate corner influence by beginning with the value a lot's side-street frontage would have if it were 100 feet deep and without corner influence and multiplying by:

25% if the main frontage is 10 ft.	58% for a 40-ft.-wide lot	70% for an 80-ft.-wide lot
40% for a 20-ft.-wide lot	63% for a 50-ft.-wide lot	71% for a 90-ft.-wide lot
51% for a 30-ft.-wide lot	68% for a 60-ft.-wide lot	72% for a 100-ft.-wide lot.

It is possible to use depth factors "backward" to find the indicated value of an inside lot if the value of an otherwise comparable corner lot is known.

As indicated earlier, highest and best use has a great deal to do with whether corner influence is important. Corner location in a rural setting can be a matter of little importance, while corner influence in a busy retail area can be of extraordinary importance. Just a few decades ago, subdivision developers, brokers, and appraisers often added a flat 10 percent or more for residential lots situated at corners. Now, corner locations in a great many residential subdivisions are no longer so strongly preferred and are often valued and priced at the same amounts as otherwise comparable *inside* lots. Such obvious advantages as more light and air and more flexibility for development were found to be offset by negative factors such as less width at the building line, more traffic, greater maintenance, and higher improvement assessments. Many developers of residential lots have found very strong market acceptance for lots on cul-de-sacs—which lots not only lack corner influence but have relatively poor frontage-to-area ratios as well. Presumably, they see advantages in terms of greater safety (fewer autos passing, at slower speeds) and often in somewhat larger land areas. These market attitudes should encourage one to question the applicability of standard-depth tables and of corner-influence tables in these neighborhoods.

The validity (and general applicability) of depth tables is obviously open to serious question. In the absence of convincing proof that the assumptions implicit in a particular depth table apply in a particular submarket, how can you justify using it? For example, why should you adopt an assumption that beneficial corner influence cannot extend over 100 feet along either street? Percentages purported to be the amount of corner influence can vary substantially from table to table. Which table to use in a particular submarket—if indeed any precomputed table does apply—can only be reliably judged from an analysis of data in that submarket. The responsible real estate professional will not willingly substitute a table of questionable applicability for detailed market analysis. (Usually, a corner lot with income-producing potential can be convincingly valued by comparison with similar lots involved in recent arms-length transactions, or by capitalization of income imputable to the site, or by both methods.)

The author does not want to overstate the case against the use of corner-influence tables. Through adequate analysis of data, some can be shown to be generally applicable in particular cases and then can be adopted as useful tools *in those cases.* The widest use of corner-influence tables is among real estate tax assessors who must be able to develop value figures for great numbers of lots and demonstrate that they have done so by some consistent procedure.

One might reasonably observe that some of these tables must have merit to have been so widely accepted. However, one might also observe that when some of the more popular tables were originated, it was common to sell patent medicines and corrective eyeglasses without individual examinations. One could draw a fair parallel between this and applying figures from a table without an examination of the submarket.

CORNER VALUE ENHANCEMENT
FOR RETAIL DISTRICTS

Ratio of main street value (front feet) to side street value (front feet)	20 × 100 ft.	30 × 100 ft.	40 × 100 ft.	50 × 100 ft.	60 × 100 ft.	70 × 100 ft.	80 × 100 ft.	90 × 100 ft.	100 × 100 ft.
10 to 1	27%	22%	18%	15%	13%	12%	11%	10%	9%
10 to 2	35	27	21	19	16	15	14	13	12
10 to 3	42	34	26	23	20	19	17	16	14
10 to 4	50	**40**	32	28	25	23	21	19	17
10 to 5	60	49	38	33	30	28	25	23	20
10 to 6	72	58	46	40	35	32	31	27	25
10 to 7	84	69	54	48	42	39	37	32	29
10 to 8	100	82	65	56	51	46	44	38	34
10 to 9	118	95	76	66	59	54	51	45	40
10 to 10	137	110	88	77	68	63	59	52	50

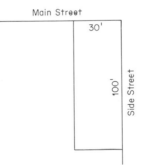

Example: Without corner influence, frontage along Main Street is worth $1,000 per front foot, and frontage along Side Street is worth $400 per front foot. Using above table, corner lot may be valued at:

Main street frontage from market (without corner influence, 30 front feet @ $1,000) — $30,000

Add corner influence from table (for 30-foot wide corner lot with 10 to 4 ratio: 40 percent of $30,000) — 12,000

$42,000

CORNER-INFLUENCE TABLE FOR COMMERCIAL LOTS

Frontage on best street	Percent of side street value to be added	Frontage on best street	Percent of side street value to be added
5 ft.	13%	55 ft.	57%
10	22	60	58
15	30	65	59
20	36	70	60
25	40	75	61
30	45	80	62
35	48	85	63
40	50	90	64
45	53	95	65
50	55	100	65

Example: Without corner influence, frontage to standard depth (100 ft.) along Main Street is worth $1,000 per front foot, and frontage along Side Street is worth $300 per front foot. Using above table, corner lot may be valued at:

30 front feet on Main @ $1,000 × 100% (standard depth) =	$30,000
100 front feet on Side @ $400 × 45% (percent taken from table for 30 ft.)	18,000
	$48,000

24   Plottage rules

A few decades ago, a flat 10 percent was often added for plottage value.

However, by now, most real estate professionals have learned that this old rule of thumb isn't at all dependable.

Sometimes when two or more sites are combined, the resultant parcel is worth more than all of the sum of the individual values before. This is because the utility per square foot or per front foot may be increased by the merging. If so, the increase in value (because of the change in utility) is called "plottage value." This is most often noted in business districts where larger-than-typical sites may be particularly prized because they are suitable for some uses which might otherwise require difficult and costly land assembly programs.

In actual assembly programs, one may cite examples of plottage value ranging from nothing to more than 100 percent. It would be a mistake to believe that utility (and unit value) is necessarily enhanced every time there is an assembly program. If one assembles a tract which is much larger than individual sites considered functional in a neighborhood, it is possible to suffer *diminution* in unit value (to the extent of all of the likely costs involved with dividing the tract into more marketable parcels and selling them off).

Neither the once-popular 10 percent allowance for plottage nor any other flat allowance is reliable. Since plottage value results from a change in utility, any rule of thumb for estimating plottage value directly must be viewed very skeptically. In estimating the value of the enlarged parcel (which would include the plottage value, if there is any), there just is no acceptable substitute for analyzing market data comparables in each case and analyzing income potential in some cases.

In every chapter in Part II, the admonition has been the same: It's too risky to rely on any of these rules of thumb—which supposedly relate various lot factors to lot values—without first proving that that rule of thumb has sound application in the particular submarket under study. Perhaps this point can be made more effectively with a hypothetical example:

You have offered to sell a sizable corner site which you own in Chicago's Loop. A prospective purchaser tries to persuade you that your price is much too high. His method, which incorporated several of these rules of thumb for lots, was as follows:

1. He started with the price paid for a nearby inside site one-third as deep as yours, . . .

2. applied a depth factor based on the 1866 Hoffman Rule, . . .

3. added corner influence from the pre-1900 work of W. A. Somers, and . . .

4. added 10 percent for plottage.

Are you convinced?

EXAMPLES OF PLOTTAGE

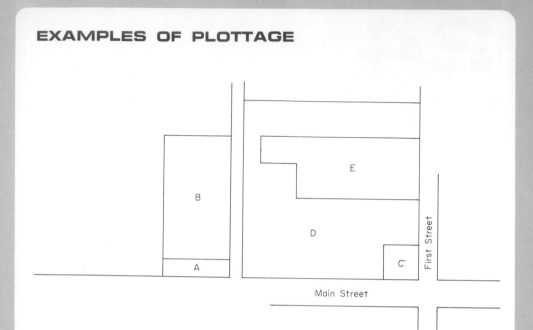

· A is too small to be buildable by itself. B lacks street frontage. Merged, they make a more functional (buildable) site.

· C's location at a prominent corner cannot be fully exploited because C is too small. D has long frontages and a large area, but it has an awkward shape and lacks corner influence. E has exposure only to one (secondary) street and no corner influence. The three sites are assembled into a large, regular, corner site with potential for a development that was not possible without unity.

Part III

Houses and Condominiums

We shape our dwellings, and afterwards our dwellings shape us.
—WINSTON CHURCHILL

2.5 times annual income

Perhaps the most widely known of all real estate rules of thumb is this: The average buyer can afford to spend about 2.5 times his annual income for a home.

There are several good indications that a lower multiple might be wiser now.

The dissemination and use of this 2.5-times-income rule of thumb have been extraordinary. Millions of persons have been exposed to it in magazine and newspaper articles. Thousands of lenders have used this rule—often in a somewhat modified form—as one of the tests in considering mortgage loan applications.

Its popularity over several decades is not hard to understand. It treats a subject of interest to most people. It is very simple to apply. It has had some basis in fact.

However, there are some important indications that a somewhat lower average multiplier may be more appropriate now. Other (nonhousing) obligations have been growing at a faster rate than effective income for the typical family, leaving a smaller percentage of income available for housing and other purchases. Relatively high interest rates in the 1970s have further strained "affordability." Many lenders have adopted multipliers on the order of 2.0 to 2.2.*

According to both public and private housing data, the average multiplier is substantially less than 2.5.

Each year, the Federal Housing Administration has been providing insurance on mortgage loans to enable a few hundred thousand families to purchase or refinance single-family dwellings worth several billion dollars. In this summary of experience in selected years, we can readily see that the average multiplier reflected by these data† is well below 2.5:

---

* That is, 2.2 × effective annual income before payments to other installment obligations or to taxes.

† Notes: Source: U.S. Department of Housing and Urban Development. Large sampling of data on one-family homes. Buyers' effective income is FHA's estimate of the mortgagor's earning capacity (before deductions for federal income taxes) that is likely to prevail during approximately the first third of the mortgage term.

To some extent this summary is probably biased by transactions involving relatively small down payments; mortgage loan amounts in these cases averaged more than 90 percent. (By contrast with this, loan-to-price ratios of conventional mortgage loans made by savings and loan associations in the late 1960s and early 1970s averaged less than 80 percent according to data from the Federal Home Loan Bank Board.) With "more typical" down payments, these same home buyers could have acquired more valuable homes, and this would have resulted in larger multipliers (still, however, below the 2.5 typical multiplier).

		Average cost of home	÷	Average buyers' total effective annual income	=	Multiplier
	1960	$14,662	÷	$ 7,584	=	1.9
New Homes	1965	16,825	÷	8,349	=	2.0
	1970	23,056	÷	12,745	=	1.8
	1960	$13,284	÷	$ 7,243	=	1.8
Existing Homes	1965	15,037	÷	8,147	=	1.8
	1970	17,959	÷	11,342	=	1.6

If, in these same FHA cases, we deducted other obligations from the buyers' income before dividing income into the cost of the home, the multiplier would naturally be somewhat higher:

		Average home price	÷	Average buyers' total effective income less other recurring charges	=	Multiplier
	1960	$14,662	÷	$ 6,894	=	2.1
New Homes	1965	16,825	÷	7,354	=	2.3
	1970	23,056	÷	11,116	=	2.1
	1960	$13,284	÷	$ 6,571	=	2.0
Existing Homes	1965	15,037	÷	7,130	=	2.1
	1970	17,959	÷	9,799	=	1.8

If we were to go one step further and also deduct taxes from effective income,* the resultant multipliers reflected by these same cases would approximate the multiplier in the rule of thumb as originally stated above:

		Average cost of home	÷	Average buyers' "net effective income"	=	Multiplier
	1960	$14,662	÷	$6,054	=	2.4
New Homes	1965	16,825	÷	6,550	=	2.6
	1970	23,056	÷	9,244	=	2.5
	1960	$13,284	÷	$5,767	=	2.3
Existing Homes	1965	15,037	÷	6,338	=	2.4
	1970	17,959	÷	8,287	=	2.2

* Ibid. From FHA's estimate of buyers' total effective income, estimated average taxes and other recurring charges were subtracted.

However, these multipliers were derived on the basis of "net" income rather than on the basis of "gross" income.

As with most rules of thumb, much of the appeal of this rule of thumb is in its simplicity. So is much of the risk involved in its use. Circumstances vary radically from prospective home buyer to prospective home buyer. How old is the principal wage earner? What is the nature of his employment? How good are his future prospects? What other sources of income does he have? What nonhousing obligations is he responsible for? How many dependents does he have? How much of a down payment will he make? What is the price range?*

In addition to these "people variables," there are also other variables to be considered. Examples:

a. Mortgage loan interest rates can make a big difference in affordability. (Say a home buyer is to repay a $35,000 loan over 30 years. The monthly payment to principal and interest is almost 20 percent higher with a 10 percent rate than with an 8 percent rate.)

b. The term of the mortgage loan also can make a big difference in affordability. (Say a home buyer is to borrow $35,000 with interest at 9 percent. The monthly payment to principal and interest is almost 12 percent higher with a 20-year term than with a 30-year term.)

c. The real estate tax burden can vary radically between two houses of the same value. (See Chapter 59.)

d. Utility costs, maintenance costs, and hazard insurance premiums can vary between houses of comparable value.

The cumulative effect of such individual differences can be quite large.

Study of the relationship between typical effective incomes and typical home purchase prices can be very useful. In addition to providing a preliminary check on affordability for the real estate broker and home buyer and serving as one of the tools of the mortgage loan reviewer, knowledge of this relationship can be very helpful in planning. For example, a developer considering erecting condominium units to sell for $25,000 should be interested to know—among other things—how many potential home buyers there are in his submarket with effective annual incomes in the range of ($25,000 ÷ say 1.7 to 2.5) say, from $10,000 to $14,700.

---

* There is a demonstrable tendency for those in higher income brackets to spend smaller percentages of their income for housing and other necessities and higher percentages for "discretionary" products and services.

26 One-fourth of income to PITI

Experienced mortgage lenders rely much more on this test—or a variation of it: In most cases, monthly mortgage payments (including real estate taxes and hazard insurance) should not exceed 25 to 35 percent of the borrower's regular income after regular payments to other important obligations have been subtracted. (Federal income taxes are not deducted.)

Each year, thousands of mortgage lenders use this standard or a modification of it in approving—or disapproving—millions of applications for home mortgage loans. They know that some families can manage larger mortgage loan payments than this; but they also have learned that, other things being generally equal, the risk of delinquencies and defaults increases when this relationship is strained.

In applying this standard in individual cases, these mortgage loan underwriters encounter many variables. One good example: They know that the typical $50,000-per-year executive will not be willing to spend nearly so high a percentage of his income as the typical $8,000-per-year wage earner.

On page 80 is an excellent example of how this rule of thumb is often applied. In this example:

a. "Total allowable monthly income" was estimated at $1,442.00.

b. From this, monthly payments on other indebtedness were deducted, leaving a net allowable monthly income of $1,319.00.

c. The projected monthly mortgage payment was:

Principal and interest:	$228.64
1/12 annual hazard insurance premium	27.12
1/12 annual real estate tax	99.24
Total monthly mortgage payment	$355.00

d. This monthly mortgage payment was less than 25 percent of the applicant's allowable monthly income (before deduction of other obligations) and less than 35 percent of the monthly income remaining after payments to other important obligations were subtracted. This was a success story: the Robinsons got their loan.

Many lenders still consider 25 percent of regular net monthly income* to be something of a desirable norm or par and approve loan applications reflecting higher percentages only in those cases in which other relationships appear

---

* That is, monthly income after payments to regular long-term obligations such as auto loans but without deduction for income taxes.

strong. In effect, that's the test illustrated here. The savings and loan association using this form might consider the Robinsons as marginal applicants.

NAME *Robinson, Jerome I. & Ruth A.*

TYPE OF LOAN	Cons	Assum	Imp	Ref	Purchase

AMOUNT AND TERMS $ _29,000_   _25_   years _8_   % _1½_ Pts.

PRINCIPAL AND INTEREST $_____228.64_____

Taxes $_____99.24_____

Insurance $_____27.12_____

Total $_____355.00_____

Multiply 48 x total = $_____17,040.00_____

Multiply 12 x monthly payments $_____1,476.00_____

Minimum Salary $_____18,516.00_____

Present Salary _12x($817 + $625)_ $_____17,304.00_____

A variation of this rule of thumb is that the monthly mortgage payment should not exceed one week's regular income after adjustment to reflect periodic payments to other important indebtedness. This variation is a little more restrictive or conservative; one week's income is equivalent to approximately 23 percent of one month's income.

Here is a sampling of FHA experience*:

		Average monthly mortgage payment	÷	Average buyers' effective income per month less other recurring obligations	=	Percentage of monthly income
	1960	$105		$576		18%
New Homes	1965	117		613		19
	1970	207		937		22
	1960	$ 99		$549		18%
Existing Homes	1965	112		594		19
	1970	171		816		21

* Average monthly mortgage payment related to average monthly income.

Source: U.S. Department of Housing and Urban Development. Large sampling of data on one-family homes with mortgage loans insured under Section 203. Federal taxes not deducted from income. Bases for FHA's estimates not entirely consistent with bases discussed for this rule of thumb.

MORTGAGE LOAN ANALYSIS

CONVENTIONAL MORTGAGE APPLICATION REVIEW
AND FIRM APPROVAL

BRANCH _Indianapolis_   BUYER _Robinson, J.I. + R.A. h/w_

LOAN # _74-437C_   P.M.I. BY _—_

INCOME: COMMENTS ON INCOME:

Principal Wage Earner $ _817.00_   _Same employment 5½ years._

OT/Bonus   @____ % $ _nominal_   _Stable emp. history._

Wife's Income @ _100_ % $ _625.00_   _Age: 43 Professional. In_
same employment almost

Other Income @____ % $ _nominal_   _18 years._

Other Income @____ % $_____

Other Income @____ % $_____

Total Allowable Monthly Income $ _1,442.00_

Long Term Obligations (10 mos. or more) $ _123.00_

INCOME RATIO #1
  a) Effective Allowable Monthly Income ($ _1,319.00_) = $ _3.72_
           Total Mortgage Payment ($ _355.00_)

  b) FNMA: 25% Total Allowable Monthly Income $ _360.50_

  c) R. R.: 2.2 x Gross Annual Income $ _38,069.00_

INCOME RATIO #2
  Net T.A.M.I x 35% (FNMA 33%) $ _504.70_

Long Term Obligations + Total Mortgage Payment $ _478.00_

A.O.P.____ V.O.E. _✓_ Card _✓_ E.M. _$1,000.00_   Appr. Value _$37,500.00_

Cert. ____ Rate _8 %_   Sale Price _36,750.00_

_25_ Yrs. _1½_ Pts. Loan Amt. _29,000.00_

This form is used by a major mortgage banking firm with ten offices in four states. Since this firm originates residential mortgage loans for later sale—often in large blocks—to insurance companies, banks, savings and loan associations, and other financial institutions, adherence to standards which are generally acceptable to such institutions is essential.

In addition to the 25-percent-of-gross-allowable-income test and the 35-percent-of-net-allowable-income test, note use of the 2.2-times-annual-income test which was discussed in the preceding chapter.

The Old Rule of 100: In buying a home, typical families can afford to spend about one hundred times what they are paying in rent.

The attraction of this rule apparently depended more upon its simplicity than upon its accuracy.

The idea that a family accustomed to paying rent of $200 per month could afford to buy a home costing about $20,000* is indeed a simple one, but one must doubt its validity in those recent decades in which sale prices often averaged more than 120 times the likely monthly housing expense.†

Curiously, it appears that this old rule may have become more valid in recent years after it had lost much of its currency. At least we know that the relationship between house prices and the expenses of living in those houses has been changing. FHA‡ and VA§ experience data in the early 1970s showed that the average home price was between 86 and 100 times the likely monthly housing expense in

* Of course, an important variable was the agreement between landlord and tenant about who paid for utilities and maintenance. Shifting of these burdens from one to the other could make a big difference in this multiplier. So could the availability of a large down payment.

† For one example, let us look at FHA Section 203 averages for new homes in 1955. The average sale price of $12,113 was almost 124 times the projected housing expense of $98.02 per month which included payments to principal and interest, mortgage insurance premium, real estate taxes, hazard insurance, maintenance and repairs, and heating and other utilities.

‡ Average sale price related to likely monthly housing expense:

		Average sale price	÷	Projected average monthly housing expense	=	Multiplier
New Homes	1970	$23,056		$246		93.7
	1971	23,835		249		95.7
	1972	24,788		256		96.8
	1973	24,672		254		97.1
Existing Homes	1970	$17,959		$208		86.3
	1971	18,980		214		88.7
	1972	19,769		221		89.5
	1973	18,948		217		87.3

Source: HUD. Large sampling of data on one-family transactions involving FHA loans issued under Section 203.

§ In 1972, the average conventional (nonmobile) home price of $23,012 was 95.5 times the average projected housing expense of $733 per month, and 73 percent of these cases involved purchase of existing structures.

that home. However, this does not necessarily provide convincing support for the Old Rule of 100. Of these home buyers who were already renting, many—probably most—were, in addition to paying rent, providing some important share of their own utilities. Further, many were "stepping up" from apartments to dwellings which were significantly better and more costly per month.

Most of the multipliers in a sizable sampling* of data in mortgage loan applications of tenants buying new homes fell within a range of 100 to 120. This will not surprise the reader who is familiar with data summarized in the next chapter.

---

* Though made on a random basis, this sampling did not have some of the essentials of a statistically random sampling.

The New Rule of 100

The New Rule of 100: A large percentage of modern condominium units are selling for something between 100 and 120 times their fair monthly rental values.

Some condominium units were designed and built as condominium units and have never been offered for rent. Some have been converted from rental units. Each time a condominium is sold, one may study the relationship between that unit's sale price and its rental value (its former rental if consistent with the market, or its fair rental *potential* as indicated by comparable rentals).

It should be stressed that we are talking about typical commercial monthly rental on an unfurnished basis with the landlord providing most of the maintenance and the tenant providing most of the utilities. We are *not* talking about rentals for furnished units, weekly or monthly seasonal rates in resort areas, or rates for former hotel rooms.

The premise here is a simple one: in the past few years,* sales of most modern and competitive condominium units have reflected gross monthly multipliers in the 100 to 120 range. Condominium units which were older or otherwise less competitive tended to reflect lower multiples. Over a three-year period in the 1970s, the author inspected 27 new condominium projects in five states. Well over 90 percent of the arm's-length transfers of individual units appeared to fall within the range of from 100 to 120 times fair monthly rental values. In communities where the condominium form of ownership was better established and where there were several projects to choose from, gross rent multipliers tended to be lower, near 100.

With the help of professionals specializing in the conversion of existing apartment projects to condominiums, the author reviewed data on more than 40 projects which were substantially sold out after 1970. Ruling out certain atypical sales,† over 80 percent of the sales reflected gross rent multipliers between 100 and 120. Some of the balance were on the low side,‡ but most of the exceptions were above 120.§

* In the United States, most of the sales of modern condominium units have taken place since 1970.

† For example, transactions involving several condominium units sold to a single investor were excluded.

‡ Cf those relatively few transactions reflecting gross rent multipliers under 100, most were accounted for by sales of converted apartments to tenants on an "as is" basis and by transactions with promotional discounts to the first few "outside" buyers.

§ In some communities, these converted apartment projects were the first condominiums, so some expensive "pioneering" was involved, and there was no competition from other condominiums. In some cases, the apartment projects were of such quality and prestige that they were clearly super-adequate for commercial apartments but were well suited to condominium conversion, and the apartment owners may not have recognized their value for conversion as well as did the purchasers who subsequently converted them.

Here is another way of saying the same thing: A large percentage of buyers of modern condomimium units are paying prices that give them a potential gross annual rental of 10 to 12 percent of the price. (This is equivalent to a monthly gross rent multiplier of 100 to 120.) In fact, this relationship has been noted a number of times. Because of market competition, this general relationship appears to exist even though many of the purchasers of individual condominium units—who are primarily interested in amenities rather than in rental income—may not be aware of it. (Some more typical considerations of these purchasers are discussed in the next chapter.)

This interesting rule of thumb has some useful applications. Several condominium converters already use it in their preliminary tests of feasibility. Real estate counselors and other specialists can use it as one of the tools in estimating demand for condominiums in specific submarkets. Appraisers can use it as an additional check on value estimates. However, this rule of thumb should never take the place of development of gross rent multipliers in a particular case if data are available in that particular submarket.

29 Sale prices of condominium units vs. value as apartments

The aggregate of sale prices of all the units in a well-planned new condominium project will typically be much more than the value of the same real estate as a commercial apartment project. Often the value as an apartment project will be from 70 to 75 percent of what the same units will sell for as condominium units.

There are several good reasons why this is so:

1. It normally costs more to build a condominium project than an apartment project. Among the increased amenities one often finds in condominium projects are lower density, more landscaping, better features in the floor plans, and more and better appliances.

2. Often, these increased amenities contribute relatively little to rental potential but increase expenses such as grounds maintenance and real estate taxes.

3. It costs a lot to sell off condominium units. If a developer has just completed 100 condominium units which can be sold off to 100 buyers over the period of a year at $25,000 each, the value of what he has right now is substantially less than (100 units @ $25,000) $2.5 million. Normally, there will be substantial sales expenses, title and transfer costs, carrying costs, delays and uncertainties. In normal circumstances, a well-informed and prudent buyer would require a large "discount" from the $2.5 million figure.

   To an extent, this situation is analogous to all of the detached dwellings in a subdivision being held under a single ownership. Assume that a speculative builder has just completed 20 single-family dwellings. A well-informed real estate broker has offered to purchase all of these homes and assume the costs and risks of selling them off to individual buyers. Naturally, he will encounter delays and costs, and he hopes to make a profit. Therefore, he needs a sizable margin or markup. What he pays the speculative builder (let's assume that it is consistent with present worth) is substantially less than these 20 homes are likely to bring when sold to individual buyers.

Lenders who provide funds for construction of new condominium projects often ask their appraisers to include estimates of the value of each project as a commercial apartment project, assuming that:

a. Construction is 100 percent complete with no changes in plans and specifications.

b. Not one unit has been sold off.

c. All of the land and improvements have been committed to use as a commercial rental project.

85

These assumptions are not at all consistent with assumptions on which the appraiser normally values a well-planned new condominium project. However, one can readily understand a lender's interest in an "upset value."* (Assuming the project doesn't win enough market acceptance to make a go of it as a condominium project, let's see what it would be worth as a commercial apartment project. When sales of condominium units lagged in the 1970s, several developers and interim lenders did in fact become landlords for a time.)

The same general premise is valid for condominium conversions as well, but the difference between the two figures is often greater; a gross margin or markup of 33⅓ percent† is considered a normal minimum spread by several experienced condominium converters. One of the reasons is that some repairs, replacements, and alterations are normally needed.

In some cases, tax considerations may figure in the spread as well. A developer-investor may be trading the sheltered income of an apartment project for ordinary income in condominium sales.

---

* Even so, these assumptions are sometimes a little too harsh. Sizable condominium projects are often developed in phases, and one of the purposes of phasing construction is to enable the developer to test market reactions and respond to them. Further, one should not totally dismiss the possibility that modifications could be made after construction has been completed in order to improve profitability as an apartment project.

† Of the anticipated aggregate of the sale prices of individual condominium units.

30 Margins for condominium conversions

Experienced condonimium converters advise against paying more for a suitable apartment project than two-thirds of what the condominium units are likely to sell for.

The difference of at least 33⅓ percent is considered by many the minimum spread in most cases to provide for repairs and replacements, improvements, promotion and sales costs, transfer expenses, net carrying costs, and net profit. Net profit requirements vary from converter to converter, but some aim for at least 20 percent of the original purchase price. Of course, costs of conversion can vary from case to case, but here we are talking about a realistic minimum spread (or gross profit requirement) in the typical case. (See also the discussion in the preceding chapter.)

31 Apartments best suited for conversion

In most markets, higher-priced condominium units (say those priced over $25,000) are a better "bet" than the lower-priced condominium units.

Here are three closely related premises:

a. Experienced condominium converters have advised against converting lower-priced projects.

b. Usually it is easier to "pioneer" higher-priced condominium units in a community.

c. Market demand factors in most markets favor the higher-priced condominium units—whether new units or converted units.

Not everyone is attracted to condominium living, but the shift in this direction in the 1970s has been dramatic.

One can combine some benefits of home ownership (a feeling of owning one's own home* and tax advantages) with some advantages of apartment living (considerable freedom from maintenance cares, more intensive use of costly land, and the sharing of costly recreational facilities).

There are reasons to believe that some of these advantages of condominium living may have greater appeal to those in high income brackets than to those in lower income brackets. For example, costs of occupying a condominium unit can be substantially less than rent for a similar apartment because of tax shelter. (See page 90.) Tax shelter is likely to have more appeal for one earning $30,000 per year than for one earning $7,000 per year.

Several other market factors should also be considered, including these:

1. Home ownership is much more prevalent among higher-income families.

2. Higher-income families are much more likely to hire others to do at least part of their home maintenance work.

3. An important percentage of purchasers of condominium units are the so-called empty nesters, couples whose children have grown. Many of these empty nesters are relatively affluent. In the latest U.S. census, over half of the couples earning over $15,000 per annum were over 45 years of age.

4. In many market areas, the least costly condominium units, the one-bedroom units, have had the weakest market acceptance; even empty nesters usually prefer a guest room or den.

* Satisfying a territorial imperative, if you like.

5. Other quality features have also proven important. In several areas, buyers have shown marked preferences for reasonable variations in architectural treatment, units which are not situated under or over another unit if in a garden-type development, individual outside areas,* adequate storage, adequate on-site parking, and other quality attributes. Some conversions and developments of condominium units lacking important quality attributes have become severe tests of the staying power of the principals.

The first step in any condominium development or conversion should be a feasibility study.† Nothing in the foregoing discussion should be substituted for a detailed study of market factors for each project. Rather, this material simply suggests several of the many factors which should be considered in each particular case.

---

* Private balconies or private patio areas or both.

† And this should be the final step if the results of this study are not favorable. (See Chapter 65.)

CONDOMINIUM SUMMARY

...joy your
...n private bath.
8. The two bedrooms in the rear are convenient to the second full bath. Each of them is bright and spacious and the closet space, once again, is more than ample. If you don't need three full-time bedrooms, either one would make a particularly nice combination sitting room/guest room.

and air condition...
closed space for laundry c...
Grabill custom kitchen cabin...
Two-door refrigerator and range
Dishwasher and sink disposer • Carport with storage section plus parking space for second car • Carefully selected lighting fixtures • Private terrace with planting area • Carpeting • Wood-burning fireplace •

onto a
...e which
...living and
...e's also space
...area that will
...ke pride in but
...pleasure to care
...st on the other
...there's another
...ea at the far end

...room to serve
...a utility room
...your laundry

...room is large
...sk or easy chairs
...ir bedroom furni-
...et defies cramming
...e size of your ward-
...l more storage space

hurst
iniums

Costs only $216.63 per month — Save $168.37

I. GROSS MONTHLY PAYMENTS		
(a) First Mortgage of $31,410.00		
for 29 years at 7.5% Interest	$221.68	
(b) Maintenance Fee	34.90	
(c) Real Estate Taxes	46.00	$302.58
II. LESS FEDERAL INCOME DEDUCTION		
For Real Estate Taxes of $46.00		
and Interest of $196.31 x 25%		(60.58)
III. LESS EQUITY BUILD-UP		(25.37)
IV. NET MONTHLY PAYMENT		$216.63
V. COMPARED TO THE PRESENT RENTAL VALUE OF		385.00
VI. MEANS A MONTHLY SAVINGS OF		$168.37

Brochures for condominium projects—whether new projects or conversions—often include summaries something like this one to emphasize lower occupancy cost because of tax shelter. (Interest and property taxes are deductible.)

Usually omitted from such summaries are provisions for such factors as anticipated appreciation or depreciation in value and provision for a reasonable return on the owner's investment in the condominium unit which would not have been required for a similar apartment unit.

 **The best time to buy a home**

The best time to buy a home: Usually it's right now.

Every year, newspaper articles tell you that right now is the best time to buy a home. With certain qualifications, this advice is usually sound—even if the people quoted in the article (builders, brokers, and lenders) often have some special interest in spurring house sales.

If you are going to buy a home sooner or later, if you plan to live there for an extended period, and if you can afford to buy now, waiting for a drop in prices or interest rates probably is not a good gamble.

Perhaps this parable will help you see why:

> **Year No. 1:** Mr. and Mrs. Smith found a new home just right for them, priced at $40,000. A 100 percent mortgage loan was available with level payments over 30 years, and interest at 10 percent. The Smiths decided they would wait for interest rates to come down.

> **Year No. 2:** Interest rates did come down—to 9 percent. (Meantime, the price of building Smith's dream house rose by 10 percent.) The Smiths decided to wait one more year to see if rates might come down still further.

> **Year No. 3:** Interest rates fell to 8 ½ percent; and 100 percent, 30-year loans were still available. The Smiths decided to buy.

> Was this a happy ending? Hardly. Prices had risen another 6 percent. As you can see here, the Smiths were actually losing ground all along. The monthly payment hasn't gotten much larger, but the (interest) portion of that payment which is tax deductible is now much smaller.

	Year no. 1	Year no. 2	Year no. 3
Price of Smith's dream home	$40,000	$44,000	$46,640
Mortgage loan interest rate	10%	9%	8$^{1}/_{2}$%
Monthly payment (principle + interest)	$351.03	$354.03	$358.62

> Even though they lost ground by waiting, the Smiths were lucky that interest rates *did* go down. If the rate had not fallen, or if it had declined more gradually, the delay could have been much more costly.

Suppose you go ahead and secure a mortgage loan at today's interest rates and buy a home, either new or existing. If rates go up, you aren't hurt. If they go down, you may want to refinance if terms of your present mortgage permit it and if the costs of refinancing aren't prohibitive. Even if the rate declines and it isn't feasible to refinance, you still may be ahead of the game—as the Smiths would have been.

On the next page are indexes of the typical costs to develop lots and houses. It's not just the fact that each index is larger than the one before it that's so troubling; it's the growing rate of increase in more recent years.

However, if we are inclined to think that rising home prices is purely a *modern* problem (or opportunity), we might do well to remember Benjamin Franklin's report on one Samuel Mickle, a pessimistic old "croaker" who didn't think much of Philadelphia's future: "This man continued to live in this decaying place and to disclaim in the same strain, refusing for many years to buy a house there because all was going to destruction, and at last I had the pleasure of seeing him give five times as much for one as he might have bought it for when he first began croaking."

PRICE INDEXES OF NEW ONE-FAMILY HOUSES SOLD, INCLUDING VALUE OF LOT: 1963 TO 1973 (1987 = 100)

Year	United States	North-east	North central	South	West
1963	90.2	90.7	89.4	91.6	91.1
1964	91.1	87.4	88.4	92.4	94.0
1965	93.2	91.3	91.4	94.6	94.0
1966	96.6	95.2	96.0	97.0	97.4
1967	100.0	100.0	100.0	100.0	100.0
1968	105.1	108.2	105.7	104.0	103.4
1969	113.6	117.7	115.7	111.4	111.6
1970	117.4	124.1	116.2	116.7	114.9
1971	123.2	134.4	119.8	124.6	117.4
1972	131.0	143.8	126.6	131.1	125.5
1973	144.8	154.7	138.9	142.9	142.4

Source: U.S. Department of Commerce, Bureau of the Census.
Note: Since houses sold each year are not the identical houses sold in other years, some adjustments are needed for consistency. Data are weighted by characteristics of houses sold in 1967, and extremes in unit prices are eliminated.

Part IV

Income
Properties

Property is desirable. It is a positive good in the world. That some should be rich, shows that others may become rich, and hence it is just encouragement to industry and enterprise.
— ABRAHAM LINCOLN

 **Future, the tense that counts**

It's the future that counts.

How much cash flow can I realistically expect from this property in the next few years? What are the chances of increasing rents? Is increased competition likely? What is likely to happen to real estate tax rates? What's going to happen to the market value of this property over the next five years? What will . . . ?

All values are based upon anticipations of the future. The value of a real property is the present worth of anticipated future benefits.

The past history of a property affects its value *only to the extent that it affects the thinking of prospective buyers as to what is likely to happen in the future.* An office building's 97 percent occupancy rate over the past several years may not impress a prospective purchaser if he notes serious overbuilding of competitive new office space.

It's what real estate investors expect in the future that counts.

34 Most important future: The near future

And it's the near future that counts most.

It is often said that the three most important things about real estate are location, location, and location. In the same spirit, one could observe that the three most important things about the ownership of income properties are time, time, and time.

A clever teacher of appraisal courses makes the point this way. Imagine that you are standing in the middle of railroad tracks and looking down them into the distance. On each cross-tie is a one-dollar bill. Each dollar looks smaller and smaller the farther away it is until dollar bills, cross-ties, and railroad tracks look like almost nothing at all as they appear to converge in the distance.

That's pretty much the way it is with anticipated future income. If someone hands you one dollar right now, it's worth one dollar right now. However, if someone agrees to hand you one dollar a year from now, that promise is worth something less than one dollar right now . . . no matter how dependable the promise.

If you have one dollar today and invest it at interest, you will have more than one dollar a year from now. By contrast, a promise to pay you a dollar one year from now must be discounted in terms of present worth to reflect the loss of use of the money during the year.

Discounting on the basis of a 9 percent interest rate,* here is what a promise to pay you one dollar at some future time is worth today:

Promise of $1.00 in . . .	Today's value
5 years	65¢
10 years	42¢
15 years	27¢
20 years	18¢

Why is a promise of one dollar 20 years from today worth only 18 cents today? Wouldn't somebody be willing to buy this promise today and pay more than 18 cents for it? Not if he is well informed; as an alternative to buying this promise, he could invest his 18 cents at 9 percent simple interest compounded annually, and the 18 cents would be worth one dollar in 20 years. Such is the impact of time and compound interest.

---

* This example was based on factors for simple interest compounded annually, and other factors, including inflation, were ruled out.

Take another example. Your Uncle Kenneth recently died and willed to you and your Cousin George a leasehold interest in a choice parcel of commercial real estate. You and George each have an undivided 50 percent interest in this leasehold which is to bring in net rental income of $10,000 each year for 99 years. Say that sales of such leasehold interests typically now reflect speculative interest rates of 10 percent. Cousin George has just come to you with an offer: In lieu of just dividing the rent equally each year between you, he would be willing to receive all of the rent for the first 10 years and then let you have all the rent for the remaining 89 years. Is George doing you a favor? He is not. Even disregarding inflation, the present worth of George's right to receive the rent for the first 10 years* would be far more than the present worth of your right to receive all of the rent for the remaining 89 years.† Time and compound interest are potent.

On the next four pages are summaries of selected compound interest factors.

One cannot truly understand income properties without appreciating the importance of time, time, and time. The further income (and expenses) are deferred into the future, the less they matter in terms of present worth.

---

* Inwood coefficient of approximately 6.145 × $10,000 = present worth of approximately $61,450.

† Inwood coefficient of approximately 3.854 × $10,000 = present worth of approximately $38,540.

WHAT IS THE PRESENT WORTH OF ONE DOLLAR PER YEAR?

If paid at the end of each year for . . .	And if the time-delay factor is reflected by discounting at a true annual rate of . . .				
	5%	6%	7%	8%	9%
1 year	0.952	0.943	0.935	0.926	0.917
2	1.859	1.833	1.808	1.783	1.759
3	2.723	2.673	2.624	2.577	2.531
4	3.546	3.465	3.387	3.312	3.240
5	4.329	4.212	4.100	3.993	3.890
6	5.076	4.917	4.767	4.623	4.486
7	5.786	5.582	5.389	5.206	5.033
8	6.463	6.210	5.971	5.747	5.535
9	7.108	6.802	6.515	6.247	5.995
10	7.722	7.360	7.024	6.710	6.418
11	8.306	7.887	7.499	7.139	6.805
12	8.863	8.384	7.943	7.536	7.161
13	9.394	8.853	8.358	7.904	7.487
14	9.899	9.295	8.745	8.244	7.786
15	10.380	9.712	9.108	8.559	8.061
16	10.838	10.106	9.447	8.851	8.313
17	11.274	10.477	9.763	9.122	8.544
18	11.690	10.828	10.059	9.372	8.756
19	12.085	11.158	10.336	9.604	8.950
20	12.462	11.470	10.594	9.818	9.129
21	12.821	11.764	10.836	10.017	9.292
22	13.163	12.042	11.061	10.201	9.442
23	13.489	12.303	11.272	10.371	9.580
24	13.799	12.550	11.469	10.529	9.707
25	14.094	12.783	11.654	10.675	9.823
26	14.375	13.003	11.826	10.810	9.929
27	14.643	13.211	11.987	10.935	10.027
28	14.898	13.406	12.137	11.051	10.116
29	15.141	13.591	12.278	11.158	10.198
30	15.372	13.765	12.409	11.258	10.274
31	15.593	13.929	12.532	11.350	10.343
32	15.803	14.084	12.647	11.435	10.406
33	16.003	14.230	12.754	11.514	10.464
34	16.193	14.368	12.854	11.587	10.518
35	16.374	14.498	12.948	11.655	10.567
36	16.547	14.621	13.035	11.717	10.612
37	16.711	14.737	13.117	11.775	10.653
38	16.868	14.846	13.193	11.829	10.691
39	17.017	14.949	13.265	11.879	10.726
40	17.159	15.046	13.332	11.925	10.757
41	17.294	15.138	13.394	11.967	10.787
42	17.423	15.225	13.452	12.007	10.813
43	17.546	15.306	13.507	12.043	10.838
44	17.663	15.383	13.558	12.077	10.861
45	17.774	15.456	13.606	12.108	10.881
46	17.880	15.524	13.650	12.137	10.900
47	17.981	15.589	13.692	12.164	10.918
48	18.077	15.650	13.730	12.189	10.934
49	18.169	15.708	13.767	12.212	10.948
50	18.256	15.762	13.801	12.233	10.962

Example: You are considering buying a leasehold position which is to pay $10,000 of net income at the end of each year for 15 years. If you wish to receive a 9 percent return on your investment, how much can you afford to pay? Answer: Approximately (8.061 × $10,000) $80,610.

10%	11%	12%	13%	14%	15%	20%
0.909	0.901	0.893	0.885	0.877	0.870	0.833
1.736	1.713	1.690	1.668	1.647	1.626	1.528
2.487	2.444	2.402	2.361	2.322	2.283	2.106
3.170	3.102	3.037	2.974	2.914	2.855	2.589
3.791	3.696	3.605	3.517	3.433	3.352	2.991
4.355	4.231	4.111	3.998	3.889	3.784	3.326
4.868	4.712	4.564	4.423	4.288	4.160	3.605
5.335	5.146	4.968	4.799	4.639	4.487	3.837
5.759	5.537	5.328	5.132	4.946	4.772	4.031
6.145	5.889	5.650	5.426	5.216	5.019	4.192
6.495	6.207	5.938	5.687	5.453	5.234	4.327
6.814	6.492	6.194	5.918	5.660	5.421	4.439
7.103	6.750	6.424	6.122	5.842	5.583	4.533
7.367	6.982	6.628	6.302	6.002	5.724	4.611
7.606	7.191	6.811	6.462	6.142	5.847	4.675
7.824	7.379	6.974	6.604	6.265	5.954	4.730
8.022	7.549	7.120	6.729	6.373	6.047	4.775
8.201	7.702	7.250	6.840	6.467	6.128	4.812
8.365	7.839	7.366	6.938	6.550	6.198	4.843
8.511	7.963	7.469	7.025	6.623	6.259	4.870
8.649	8.075	7.562	7.102	6.687	6.312	4.891
8.772	8.176	7.645	7.170	6.743	6.359	4.909
8.883	8.266	7.718	7.230	6.792	6.399	4.925
8.985	8.348	7.784	7.283	6.835	6.434	4.937
9.077	8.422	7.843	7.330	6.873	6.464	4.948
9.161	8.488	7.896	7.072	6.906	6.491	4.956
9.237	8.548	7.943	7.409	6.935	6.514	4.964
9.307	8.602	7.984	7.441	6.961	6.534	4.970
9.370	8.650	8.022	7.470	6.983	6.551	4.975
9.427	8.694	8.055	7.496	7.003	6.566	4.979
9.479	8.733	8.085	7.518	7.020	6.579	4.982
9.526	8.769	8.112	7.538	7.035	6.591	4.985
9.569	8.801	8.135	7.556	7.048	6.600	4.988
9.609	8.829	8.157	7.572	7.060	6.609	4.990
9.644	8.855	8.176	7.586	7.070	6.617	4.991
9.677	8.879	8.192	7.598	7.079	6.623	4.993
9.706	8.900	8.208	7.609	7.087	6.629	4.994
9.733	8.919	8.221	7.618	7.094	6.634	4.995
9.757	8.936	8.233	7.627	7.100	6.638	4.996
9.779	8.951	8.244	7.634	7.105	6.642	4.997
9.799	8.965	8.253	7.641	7.110	6.645	4.997
9.817	8.977	8.262	7.647	7.114	6.648	4.998
9.834	8.989	8.270	7.652	7.117	6.650	4.998
9.849	8.999	8.276	7.657	7.120	6.652	4.998
9.863	9.008	8.283	7.661	7.123	6.654	4.999
9.875	9.016	8.288	7.664	7.126	6.656	4.999
9.887	9.024	8.293	7.668	7.128	6.657	4.999
9.897	9.030	8.297	7.671	7.130	6.659	4.999
9.906	9.036	8.301	7.673	7.131	6.660	4.999
9.915	9.042	8.304	7.675	7.133	6.661	4.999

WHAT IS THE PRESENT WORTH
OF ONE DOLLAR TO BE RECEIVED
AT A GIVEN TIME IN THE FUTURE?

If the dollar is to be paid at the end of . . .	And if the time-delay factor is to be reflected by discounting at a true annual rate of . . .				
	5%	6%	7%	8%	9%
1 year	0.952	0.943	0.935	0.926	0.917
2	0.907	0.890	0.873	0.857	0.842
3	0.864	0.840	0.816	0.794	0.772
4	0.823	0.792	0.763	0.735	0.708
5	0.784	0.747	0.713	0.681	0.650
6	0.746	0.705	0.666	0.630	0.596
7	0.711	0.665	0.623	0.583	0.547
8	0.677	0.627	0.582	0.540	0.502
9	0.645	0.592	0.544	0.500	0.460
10	0.614	0.558	0.508	0.463	0.422
11	0.585	0.527	0.475	0.429	0.388
12	0.557	0.497	0.444	0.397	0.356
13	0.530	0.469	0.415	0.368	0.326
14	0.505	0.442	0.388	0.340	0.299
15	0.481	0.417	0.362	0.315	0.275
16	0.458	0.394	0.339	0.292	0.252
17	0.436	0.371	0.317	0.270	0.231
18	0.416	0.350	0.296	0.250	0.212
19	0.396	0.331	0.277	0.232	0.194
20	0.377	0.312	0.258	0.215	0.178
21	0.359	0.294	0.242	0.199	0.164
22	0.342	0.278	0.226	0.184	0.150
23	0.326	0.262	0.211	0.170	0.138
24	0.310	0.247	0.197	0.157	0.126
25	0.295	0.233	0.184	0.146	0.116
26	0.281	0.220	0.172	0.135	0.106
27	0.268	0.207	0.161	0.125	0.098
28	0.255	0.196	0.150	0.116	0.090
29	0.243	0.185	0.141	0.107	0.082
30	0.231	0.174	0.131	0.099	0.075
31	0.220	0.164	0.123	0.092	0.069
32	0.210	0.155	0.115	0.085	0.063
33	0.200	0.146	0.107	0.079	0.058
34	0.190	0.138	0.100	0.073	0.053
35	0.181	0.130	0.093	0.068	0.049
36	0.173	0.123	0.088	0.063	0.045
37	0.164	0.116	0.082	0.058	0.041
38	0.157	0.109	0.076	0.054	0.038
39	0.149	0.103	0.071	0.050	0.035
40	0.142	0.097	0.067	0.046	0.032
41	0.135	0.092	0.062	0.043	0.029
42	0.129	0.087	0.058	0.039	0.027
43	0.123	0.082	0.055	0.037	0.025
44	0.117	0.077	0.051	0.034	0.023
45	0.111	0.073	0.048	0.031	0.021
46	0.106	0.069	0.044	0.029	0.019
47	0.101	0.065	0.042	0.027	0.017
48	0.096	0.061	0.039	0.025	0.016
49	0.092	0.058	0.036	0.023	0.015
50	0.087	0.054	0.034	0.021	0.013

Example: What would I pay today for the promise to pay me $100,000 20 years from today if I

10%	11%	12%	13%	14%	15%	20%
0.909	0.901	0.893	0.885	0.877	0.870	0.833
0.826	0.812	0.797	0.783	0.769	0.756	0.694
0.751	0.731	0.712	0.693	0.675	0.658	0.579
0.683	0.659	0.636	0.613	0.592	0.572	0.482
0.621	0.593	0.567	0.543	0.519	0.497	0.402
0.564	0.535	0.507	0.480	0.456	0.432	0.335
0.513	0.482	0.452	0.425	0.400	0.376	0.279
0.467	0.434	0.404	0.376	0.351	0.327	0.233
0.424	0.391	0.361	0.333	0.308	0.284	0.194
0.386	0.352	0.322	0.295	0.270	0.247	0.162
0.350	0.317	0.287	0.261	0.237	0.215	0.135
0.319	0.286	0.257	0.231	0.208	0.187	0.112
0.290	0.258	0.229	0.204	0.182	0.163	0.093
0.263	0.232	0.205	0.181	0.160	0.141	0.078
0.239	0.209	0.183	0.160	0.140	0.123	0.065
0.218	0.188	0.163	0.141	0.123	0.107	0.054
0.198	0.170	0.146	0.125	0.108	0.093	0.045
0.180	0.153	0.130	0.111	0.095	0.081	0.038
0.164	0.138	0.116	0.098	0.083	0.070	0.031
0.149	0.124	0.104	0.087	0.073	0.061	0.026
0.135	0.112	0.093	0.077	0.064	0.053	0.022
0.123	0.101	0.083	0.068	0.056	0.046	0.018
0.112	0.091	0.074	0.060	0.049	0.040	0.015
0.102	0.082	0.066	0.053	0.043	0.035	0.013
0.092	0.074	0.059	0.047	0.038	0.030	0.010
0.084	0.066	0.053	0.042	0.033	0.026	0.009
0.076	0.060	0.047	0.037	0.029	0.023	0.007
0.069	0.054	0.042	0.033	0.026	0.020	0.006
0.063	0.048	0.037	0.029	0.022	0.017	0.005
0.057	0.044	0.033	0.026	0.020	0.015	0.004
0.052	0.039	0.030	0.023	0.017	0.013	0.004
0.047	0.035	0.027	0.020	0.015	0.011	0.003
0.043	0.032	0.024	0.018	0.013	0.010	0.002
0.039	0.029	0.021	0.016	0.012	0.009	0.002
0.036	0.026	0.019	0.014	0.010	0.008	0.002
0.032	0.023	0.017	0.012	0.009	0.007	0.001
0.029	0.021	0.015	0.011	0.008	0.006	0.001
0.027	0.019	0.013	0.010	0.007	0.005	0.001
0.024	0.017	0.012	0.009	0.006	0.004	0.001
0.022	0.015	0.011	0.008	0.005	0.004	0.001
0.020	0.014	0.010	0.007	0.005	0.003	0.001
0.018	0.012	0.009	0.006	0.004	0.003	0.000
0.017	0.011	0.008	0.005	0.004	0.002	0.000
0.015	0.010	0.007	0.005	0.003	0.002	0.000
0.014	0.009	0.006	0.004	0.003	0.002	0.000
0.012	0.008	0.005	0.004	0.002	0.002	0.000
0.011	0.007	0.005	0.003	0.002	0.001	0.000
0.010	0.007	0.004	0.003	0.002	0.001	0.000
0.009	0.006	0.004	0.003	0.002	0.001	0.000
0.009	0.005	0.003	0.002	0.001	0.001	0.000

require a 10 percent return on my investment? Answer: Approximately (0.149 × $100,000) $14,900.

35

No. 1 goal of many: Cash flow

Many—perhaps most—knowledgeable buyers of major income properties have the same primary goal: Cash flow.

Increasingly, real estate professionals think of equity investments in major income properties as investments *for a limited time.* Very often, major income properties are resold before they have been held for ten years.*

Real Estate Investment Group (REIG) has just bought a $1,000,000 apartment building by arranging a new, long-term $750,000 mortgage loan and putting in $250,000 in cash. After deducting out-of-pocket operating expenses and the mortgage payments to principal and interest, there will be a significant amount of money remaining each year, much of which will be sheltered from federal income taxes in these early years by depreciation allowances. The residual cash (or cash flow or cash throw-off) will be REIG's only important reward for the $250,000 investment in early years.† To be sure, other rewards (returns) may come to Real Estate Investment Group as a result of the $250,000 investment. At the time of purchase, however, REIG gave limited weight to these possible rewards because they seemed somewhat uncertain and because they will be deferred several years into the future.‡

In recent studies,§ large majorities of the investors sampled agreed on the one investment goal that had most attracted each: cash flow.

In mid-1973, the man in charge of acquisitions for a major institutional investor spoke to a meeting of the prestigious American Society of Real Estate Counselors.

* If a form of accelerated depreciation was elected in the year of purchase, the allowable annual depreciation can taper off markedly over several years. Most purchases of major income properties involve major, long-term financing requiring regular amortization. After several years of ownership, a substantial portion of each mortgage payment is going to principal reduction (a claim on cash flow but not a deductible expense). For these and some other important reasons, many major income properties are resold before they have been held for ten years.

† Real Estate Investment Group originally put in $250,000 in cash. Each year REIG receives some cash flow. This is called the "cash-on-cash return." The rate of cash-on-cash return is a matter of keen interest to many sophisticated income property investors.

‡ The value of this property could increase over time, but this possible "reward" is not likely to be realized until the property is sold or refinanced. (Many mortgage agreements contain limitations on the borrowers' right to prepay without incurring a substantial penalty. Even if the prepayment option is open, direct and indirect costs of refinancing can be substantial.) For a discussion of how deferring benefits into the future can diminish their impact on present worth, see the preceding chapter.

§ Example: "Study on Tax Considerations in Multi-Family Housing Investments," Superintendent of Documents, Washington, D.C.

Said this recognized expert on major income properties, "We're cash flow buyers, pure and simple."*

Interview after interview with seasoned and well-informed investors in major income properties has revealed a fundamental concern with the amount and dependability of cash flow.

Most buyers of major income properties want large, long-term mortgage financing. If the amount of cash flow in early years is so very important to the investor-borrowers, one would expect many of them to be even more concerned with holding down the size of mortgage payments relative to the amount borrowed† than they are about holding down the interest rate. As we shall see in the next chapter, that is just what one finds.

* This should not be construed to mean that this man and other seasoned equity investors are not keenly interested in other possible rewards—normally deferred into the future—such as principal reduction and appreciation in value, but rather that they differentiate between likely cash income and less certain rewards.

† Most mortgage loans on major income properties require periodic payments to debt service (principal and interest), all of the same size. The total of these payments per year divided by the original principal amount of the mortgage loan is called the "annual percent constant."

36 Loan rates related to bond yields

Interest rates on large income property mortgages are closely related to bond yields.

Mortgages and bonds are similar in several ways. Both are normally regarded as long-term investments (often with penalty provisions for early payoff). By and large, both are fixed-income investments (although both sometimes have "kickers"*). Both have preferred positions in that they normally have a claim on the income stream which is prior to that of the ownership interest. To a considerable extent, these two forms of long-term financing represent investment alternatives to one another.

Thus, it is not too surprising to find that yields on mortgage loans have been paralleling bond yields. This is true for both mortgage loans on dwellings and those on major income properties.

Insurance companies have enormous amounts of money to place in long-term investments each year,† and most are invested in long-term mortgages and bonds.‡ Over one-fourth of commercial property mortgages outstanding in the United States are held by insurance companies.§

In seeking good investments in income property mortgages and in bonds, insurance companies must compete with others in the market.

Not surprisingly, there are generally consistent relationships between the yields from investment quality bonds and the interest rates on good, large income property mortgages. In recent decades, they have tended to move in parallel patterns, with bond yields being somewhat lower. This difference in yields is largely because investments in bonds can be made and looked after more cheaply and because bonds can be converted to cash more readily. However, it is worth noting that the difference between the two has narrowed somewhat in recent years, partly because the costs of originating and watching over good, large income property

---

* For example, bonds may have options to buy stock at some price that could become attractive, and mortgagees sometimes have the right to participate in future increases in income from the properties which secure the mortgages.

† In 1972 alone, U.S. life insurance companies invested (originated or purchased) over $8.2 billion in long-term mortgage loans. Source: Institute of Life Insurance.

‡ By the end of 1972, mortgages held by U.S. life insurance companies represented 32.1 percent of their total assets, and bonds represented another 35.9 percent; all of their other investments combined represented less than one-third of their assets, according to the Institute of Life Insurance.

§ Estimated figures at the end of 1972: $30.7 billion ÷ $107.5 billion = 28.6 percent. Sources: Institute of Life Insurance and Federal Reserve bulletins.

loans have been declining on a relative basis,* and perhaps partly because invest-ment experts are becoming more aware that a prime mortgage loan is a reasonably salable asset.

This comparison between average yields on those bonds placed directly with insurance companies and average interest rates set out in insurance company commitments on major income property mortgage loans leaves little doubt about the close relationship between the two.

Comparison of Yields on Investments of Life Insurance Companies

	Average interest rates on income property mortgages*	÷	Average yields on directly placed corporate bonds†	=	Factor
1966	6.35%		6.10%		1.04
1967	6.92		6.63		1.04
1968	7.65		7.45		1.03
1969	8.62		8.39		1.03
1970	9.86		10.08		0.98
1971	8.99		8.84		1.02
1972	8.50		8.40		1.01

* Dollar-weighted average of interest rates in American Life Insurance Association commitment study discussed in the next chapter.

† *Source:* Another ongoing study by American Life Insurance Association, "Average Yields on Directly Placed Corporate Bond Authorizations." This survey covers life insurance companies accounting for well over one-half of the assets of all U.S. life insurance companies. These yield averages are weighted by amounts of authorizations.

Sometimes one is a little higher, sometimes the other. But the difference between these averages has consistently been small.

It is tempting to say that this is pretty much because insurance companies base their mortgage loan underwriting not so much on the property as on the credit standing of the borrower or the credit standing of the property's tenants. (Indeed, experts in the securities department of an insurance company often give analytical advice to officers in the mortgage loan department, and some mortgage loan de-partments of major life insurance companies have even added corporate credit an-alysts.) However, this doesn't hold water. As we shall see in the next section, inter-est rates have tended to vary surprisingly little from property type to property type, and interest rates on apartment loans (consistently representing a large percent-age of income property commitments and typically based primarily upon real prop-erty values) have moved with the rest and have paralleled bond yields.

Clearly, many real estate experts closely watch movements in bond yields. Perhaps more should.

* Largely, this is a natural concomitant of a dramatically increased average loan amount.

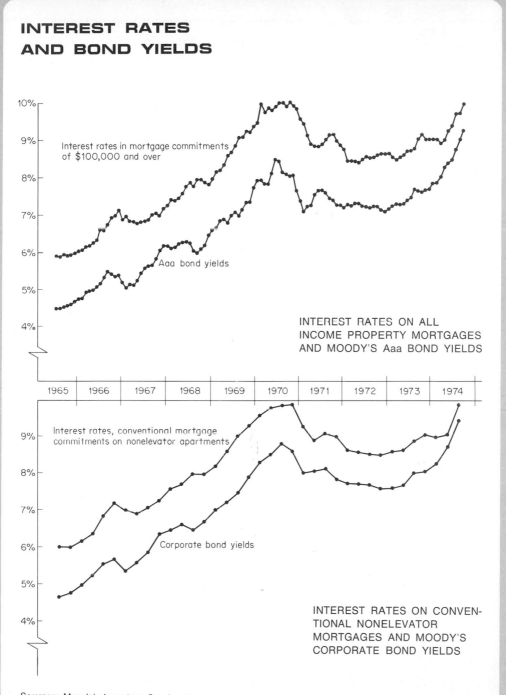

INTEREST RATES
AND BOND YIELDS

Interest rates in mortgage commitments
of $100,000 and over

Aaa bond yields

INTEREST RATES ON ALL
INCOME PROPERTY MORTGAGES
AND MOODY'S Aaa BOND YIELDS

1965 | 1966 | 1967 | 1968 | 1969 | 1970 | 1971 | 1972 | 1973 | 1974

Interest rates, conventional mortgage
commitments on nonelevator apartments

Corporate bond yields

INTEREST RATES ON CONVEN-
TIONAL NONELEVATOR
MORTGAGES AND MOODY'S
CORPORATE BOND YIELDS

Sources: Moody's Investors Service. Interest rates are averages weighted by dollar amounts from
the previously discussed ALIA study.

37 Loan interest rate vs. payment size as value determinant

Most developers and buyers of major income properties want large mortgage loans. They appear to care more about payment size than they do about interest rate.

(To say the same thing more precisely: In recent decades, the percent constants of mortgage loans on choice income properties have closely paralleled capitalization rates. Interest rates on these same loans have not.)

To be sure, interest rates on these mortgage loans are important. Mortgage loan interest is often one of the largest claims against the income from a property. Naturally, the prudent investor wants to hold down the interest cost.

However, it would be a serious mistake to assume that other mortgage loan terms are not very important also. Another factor of keen interest is the nature of the amortization. How many years will the loan run? Will all of the borrowed money have to be repaid during the term, as is most common, or will there be a "balloon" payment at the end? Will the regular payments all be of the same size, as they are in most cases?

The nut of it is this: How large are the payments to principal and interest relative to the amount borrowed? If other things are equal, a longer term of years means smaller payments and more cash flow; a shorter term means larger payments and less cash flow.* And we saw in the last two chapters how vitally important the near-term cash flow is in most cases.

Seasoned investors in large income properties usually think and talk in terms of percent constants. Say that a $1 million mortgage loan is to be repaid in level monthly payments to principal and interest, which payments total $103,000 each year. Then the percent constant (annual) is ($103,000 ÷ $1,000,000) 10.3. In other words, a 10.3 percent constant simply means that principal and interest payments each year will be equivalent to 10.3 percent of the original amount of the loan. Recognizing that the *size* of the annual debt service burden is a very important factor indeed, most major mortgage lenders and income property investors keep their percent constant tables handy.

Remember that the size of the mortgage payments is only partly determined by

---

* Of course, with a shorter term and larger payments, the indebtedness is reduced more rapidly. However, as pointed out in the preceding chapter, this usually represents a reward that will be deferred into the future.

110

the interest rate in each case. The loan term is also an important factor, as these figures clearly show:

How the Payment Size Varies with Different Interest Rates and Loan Terms

	Annual percent constant*		
Mortgage loan interest rate	(10-year Loan Term)	(20-year Loan Term)	(30-year Loan Term)
6%	13.32%	8.60%	7.20%
8	14.56	10.04	8.81
10	15.86	11.58	10.53
12	17.22	13.21	12.34

* These are slightly rounded figures for fully amortized mortgages with level monthly payments. For approximate monthly payment, divide annual percent constant by 12.

On the next page is a summary of selected figures from a very important and enlightening study of over 41,000 income property mortgage loan commitments aggregating over $44,000,000,000—yes, $44 *billion.* Despite some imprecision in the computation of nonrate terms, this voluminous and ongoing study provides us with one of the few good windows through which we may study the financing of major income properties. Mortgage loan interest rates have changed dramatically during the years of this study (tending to rather closely parallel bond yields, as we just saw in the last chapter). However, percent constants have remained much more stable because the insurance company lenders have been willing to ease maturities in the face of rising rates.* Fortunately, both lenders and borrowers were able to get something very important from these transactions despite some radical changes in capital markets: the lenders could continue to get interest rates which were reasonable in relation to yields on alternative investments, and the borrowers were able to hold down the size of their payments (percent constants) so that cash flow was adequate. Not surprisingly, the percent constants in this study have related much more closely to values which the lenders estimated for these income properties than have interest rates.†

* This is not to imply that the properties securing these loans were necessarily of quite consistent quality throughout the term of this study.

† This is hardly surprising in view of the foregoing.

Capitalization rates in this study were derived for each loan by dividing the estimate of net stabilized earnings per annum (before deductions for debt service) by the estimated property value. Since net stabilized earnings were not estimated for certain property types, such as eleemosynary institutions, the capitalization rates shown in the tables are averages of individual rates for which information was available.

One should bear in mind that capitalization rates were derived from estimates which could reflect subjective bias because of competition for attractive investments or liberal or conservative attitudes toward particular properties.

23 YEARS OF MORTGAGE COMMITMENTS ON LARGE INCOME PROPERTIES

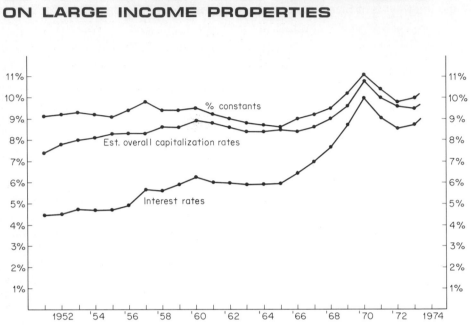

23 YEARS OF MORTGAGE COMMITMENTS ON LARGE INCOME PROPERTIES

Year	No. of loans	Total amount committed (million $)	Averages (by number of loans)			Estimated overall capitalization rate (%)
			Interest rate	Maturity years/months	Percent constant	
1951	445	171.8	4.43	15/03	9.1	7.4
1952	573	225.2	4.54	15/06	9.2	7.8
1953	730	338.1	4.76	15/11	9.3	8.0
1954	973	568.7	4.66	16/03	9.2	8.1
1955	1,204	603.7	4.66	16/04	9.1	8.3
1956	1,354	662.6	4.94	16/02	9.4	8.3
1957	938	594.1	5.65	16/02	9.8	8.3
1958	1,356	745.7	5.60	17/00	9.4	8.6
1959	1,546	902.5	5.92	17/06	9.4	8.6
1960	1,992	1,039.2	6.25	17/09	9.5	8.9
1961	2,087	1,391.2	6.04	18/04	9.2	8.8
1962	2,310	1,697.3	5.99	18/11	9.0	8.6
1963	2,699	2,158.5	5.90	19/06	8.8	8.4
1964	3,190	2,461.2	5.90	19/11	8.7	8.4
1965	3,564	3,002.9	5.95	20/02	8.6	8.5
1966	2,796	2,515.7	6.42	20/05	9.0	8.4
1967	2,726	3,027.2	6.97	21/02	9.2	8.6
1968	2,569	3,244.3	7.66	22/11	9.5	9.0
1969	1,788	2,920.7	8.69	21/08	10.2	9.6
1970	912	2,341.1	9.93	22/08	11.1	10.8
1971	1,664	3,982.5	9.07	22/10	10.4	10.0
1972	2,132	4,986.5	8.57	23/03	9.8	9.6
1973	2,140	4,833.3	8.76	23/03	10.0	9.5

These were selected from data furnished by the American Life Insurance Association for new commitments of $100,000 and over each, of selected life insurance companies. The 15 companies reporting account for more than one-half of both the total assets and the nonfarm mortgages held by all U.S. life insurance companies. Averages are weighted by number of loans. Averages for nonrate terms of these loans may represent a fewer number of loans than the number specified. Data on average percent constants is limited to cases of full amortization over the loan term and cases in which enough data were reported to enable this relationship to be estimated by ALIA. These figures exclude construction loans, increases in existing loans in a company's portfolio, reapprovals, and loans secured by land only.

ANNUAL CONSTANTS:

What Percent of the Original Loan Amount is Required for Principal and Interest Payments Each Year?

If the loan is repaid in level monthly payments over . . .	And the mortgage loan interest rate is . . .					
	6%	6¹/₂%	7%	7¹/₂%	8%	8¹/₂%
5 years	23.20	23.48	23.76	24.05	24.33	24.62
6	19.89	20.17	20.46	20.75	21.04	21.33
7	17.53	17.82	18.11	18.41	18.70	19.00
8	15.77	16.06	16.36	16.66	16.96	17.27
9	14.41	14.71	15.01	15.31	15.62	15.94
10	13.32	13.63	13.93	14.24	14.56	14.88
11	12.44	12.75	13.06	13.38	13.70	14.02
12	11.71	12.02	12.34	12.66	12.99	13.32
13	11.10	11.41	11.74	12.06	12.40	12.73
14	10.57	10.90	11.22	11.56	11.90	12.24
15	10.13	10.45	10.79	11.12	11.47	11.82
16	9.74	10.07	10.41	10.75	11.10	11.45
17	9.40	9.73	10.08	10.42	10.78	11.14
18	9.10	9.44	9.79	10.14	10.50	10.87
19	8.83	9.18	9.53	9.89	10.25	10.63
20	8.60	8.95	9.30	9.67	10.04	10.41
21	8.39	8.74	9.10	9.47	9.85	10.23
22	8.20	8.56	8.92	9.29	9.67	10.06
23	8.03	8.39	8.76	9.14	9.52	9.91
24	7.87	8.24	8.61	9.00	9.38	9.78
25	7.73	8.10	8.48	8.87	9.26	9.66
26	7.60	7.98	8.36	8.75	9.15	9.56
27	7.49	7.87	8.25	8.65	9.05	9.46
28	7.38	7.76	8.16	8.55	8.96	9.37
29	7.28	7.67	8.07	8.47	8.88	9.30
30	7.20	7.58	7.98	8.39	8.81	9.23
31	7.11	7.51	7.91	8.32	8.74	9.16
32	7.04	7.43	7.84	8.25	8.68	9.11
33	6.97	7.37	7.78	8.20	8.62	9.05
34	6.90	7.31	7.72	8.14	8.57	9.01
35	6.84	7.25	7.67	8.09	8.52	8.96
36	6.79	7.20	7.62	8.05	8.48	8.92
37	6.74	7.15	7.57	8.00	8.44	8.89
38	6.69	7.10	7.53	7.97	8.41	8.85
39	6.64	7.06	7.49	7.93	8.37	8.82
40	6.60	7.03	7.46	7.90	8.34	8.80

Example: If $100,000 is to be repaid with 9% interest in level monthly installments over 25 years, the principal and interest payments each year will aggregate approximately (10.07% of $100,000) $10,070.00, and each monthly debt service payment will be approximately ($10,070 ÷ 12) $839.17.

9%	9¹/₂%	10%	10¹/₂%	11%	12%	15%
24.91	25.20	25.50	25.79	26.09	26.69	28.55
21.63	21.93	22.23	22.53	22.84	23.46	25.37
19.31	19.61	19.92	20.23	20.55	21.18	23.16
17.58	17.89	18.21	18.53	18.85	19.50	21.53
16.25	16.57	16.89	17.22	17.55	18.22	20.31
15.20	15.53	15.86	16.19	16.53	17.22	19.36
14.35	14.69	15.02	15.37	15.71	16.41	18.61
13.66	14.00	14.34	14.69	15.04	15.76	18.01
13.08	13.42	13.77	14.13	14.49	15.22	17.52
12.59	12.94	13.30	13.66	14.03	14.78	17.12
12.17	12.53	12.90	13.26	13.64	14.40	16.80
11.81	12.18	12.55	12.93	13.31	14.08	16.52
11.51	11.88	12.25	12.64	13.02	13.81	16.29
11.24	11.61	12.00	12.39	12.78	13.58	16.10
11.00	11.39	11.78	12.17	12.57	13.38	15.94
10.80	11.19	11.58	11.98	12.39	13.21	15.80
10.62	11.01	11.41	11.82	12.23	13.06	15.69
10.45	10.85	11.26	11.67	12.09	12.94	15.59
10.31	10.72	11.13	11.54	11.96	12.82	15.50
10.18	10.59	11.01	11.43	11.86	12.72	15.43
10.07	10.48	10.90	11.33	11.76	12.64	15.37
9.97	10.39	10.81	11.24	11.68	12.56	15.32
9.88	10.30	10.73	11.16	11.60	12.50	15.27
9.80	10.22	10.66	11.09	11.54	12.44	15.23
9.72	10.15	10.59	11.03	11.48	12.39	15.20
9.66	10.09	10.53	10.98	11.43	12.34	15.17
9.60	10.03	10.48	10.93	11.38	12.30	15.15
9.54	9.98	10.43	10.88	11.34	12.27	15.13
9.49	9.94	10.39	10.84	11.30	12.24	15.11
9.45	9.90	10.35	10.81	11.27	12.21	15.09
9.41	9.86	10.32	10.78	11.24	12.19	15.08
9.37	9.83	10.29	10.75	11.22	12.17	15.07
9.34	9.80	10.26	10.72	11.19	12.15	15.06
9.31	9.77	10.23	10.70	11.17	12.13	15.05
9.28	9.74	10.21	10.68	11.16	12.12	15.04
9.26	9.72	10.19	10.66	11.14	12.10	15.04

38 Loan rates related to property types

Do interest rates on prime mortgages vary much from one type of income property to another? Less than many of us have come to expect.

Are interest rates on motel loans much higher than those on shopping centers? How do interest rates on office building mortgages compare with those on apartments?

Even some very well-informed readers are likely to find some surprises in the table on the next two pages. Differences in interest rates by property types were relatively small in the 7-year (27-quarter) sample here. This is no small sampling. These figures are averages for over 11,000 commitments aggregating over $22 billion by some of the most knowledgeable and experienced mortgage loan specialists.

MORTGAGE LOAN INTEREST RATES

Averages by Selected Property Types

		Conventional elevator apartments	Conventional nonelevator apartments	Shopping centers (5 or more stores)	Retail stores (less than 5 stores)	Office buildings	Medical office buildings
1968	I	7.58%	7.55%	7.34%	7.38%	7.30%	7.40%
	II	7.78	7.70	7.64	7.51	7.61	7.59
	III	8.00	7.98	8.00	7.98	7.83	7.71
	IV	7.99	7.96	7.91	7.87	7.87	7.89
1969	I	8.22	8.17	8.17	8.02	8.12	
	II	8.75	8.57	8.51	8.50	8.54	8.61
	III	9.03	8.99	9.19	9.07	9.00	9.02
	IV	9.18	9.19	9.62	9.53	9.30	9.31
1970	I	9.56	9.53	9.98	9.81	9.83	9.64
	II	9.76	9.71	10.29	9.86	9.97	9.67
	III	10.09	9.80	10.35	10.31	10.08	10.10
	IV	10.03	9.86	10.21	10.27	10.13	9.94
1971	I	9.18	9.19	9.39	9.17	9.43	9.31
	II	8.79	8.85	9.10	8.90	8.87	8.92
	III	9.01	9.03	9.06	9.07	9.01	9.09
	IV	8.98	9.01	8.92	9.16	9.00	9.14
1972	I	8.62	8.62	8.42	8.65	8.56	8.46
	II	8.45	8.53	8.39	8.16	8.46	8.40
	III	8.51	8.50	8.51	8.46	8.53	8.55
	IV	8.58	8.60	8.51	8.54	8.57	8.61
1973	I	8.65	8.58	8.52	8.36	8.60	8.55
	II	8.54	8.60	8.56	8.63	8.58	8.55
	III	8.94	8.87	8.70	8.79	8.72	8.85
	IV	9.05	9.09	9.05	9.10	9.07	9.08
1974	I	9.22	8.94	8.89	9.00	9.02	8.94
	II	9.20	9.07	9.18	9.19	9.13	9.07
	III	9.91	9.87	9.81	9.77	9.74	10.15

Source: Ongoing American Life Insurance Association study, "Survey of Mortgage Commitments on Nonresidential Properties Reported by 15 Life Insurance Companies."
Notes: The 15 reporting companies account for over one-half of assets and over one-half of nonfarm mortgages held by all U.S. life insurance companies. Averages in this summary are weighted by number of loans committed. Each commitment reported was $100,000 or over. The figures exclude construction loans, increases in existing loans in a company's portfolio, reapprovals, and loans secured by land only. Very few commitments were made for loans on certain property types in certain quarters, and average interest rates were not reported.

Commercial warehouse	Hospital and institutional	Nursing homes	Industrial warehouses	Manufacturing plants	Motels
7.15%	7.06%	7.35%	7.87%	7.26%	7.58%
7.54	7.41	7.40	7.58	7.54	7.80
7.82	7.34	8.00	7.93	7.93	8.12
7.87		7.97	7.81	7.85	8.20
8.21	8.15	8.35	8.14	8.08	8.12
0.50	8.52	8.54	8.68	8.60	8.65
9.28	8.83	9.33	9.08	9.16	9.19
9.83		9.19	9.41	9.47	9.75
9.97	8.80	9.70	9.79	9.85	9.56
10.33	9.75		10.52	10.20	
10.40	9.83	9.33	10.19	10.43	
10.28	9.62		10.58		
9.58	10.17	9.81	9.62	9.68	9.75
9.03	9.42	8.85	8.89	9.16	10.00
9.13	8.88	9.44	9.08	9.11	9.57
9.19	8.43	9.25	9.01	9.13	9.64
8.71	8.56	9.05	8.50	8.85	8.81
8.70	8.50	8.94	8.50	8.38	8.77
8.59	8.75	8.85	8.63	8.54	9.07
8.74		9.16	8.59	8.61	9.13
8.63	8.88	9.15	8.59	8.63	9.01
8.66	9.00	9.33	8.64	8.62	9.08
8.77	8.84	9.35	8.77	8.72	9.19
9.09		9.75	9.10	9.16	9.43
9.04		9.66	9.07	9.21	9.38
9.40	9.29	9.58	9.27	9.40	9.43
9.94		10.08	9.74	10.23	9.71

 Debt coverage factors

Debt coverage factors are very important. Lenders often require debt coverage factors in the 1.20 to 1.40 range.

In deciding if the net operating income expected from a property will be adequate to meet certain principal and interest (debt service) payments, most mortgage lenders want a safety margin or "cushion." Then, if the net operating income turns out to be a little less than expected, there will still be enough net operating income to make the mortgage payments.

Most often, this required margin is between 20 and 40 percent. It may be higher for some special-purpose properties. It is sometimes lower in cases involving long-term, net leases to blue-chip tenants in which income and expenses are likely to vary very little.

In a cursory sampling of debt coverage requirements in 1975, the author talked with 34 mortgage loan officers of commercial banks, mortgage banking firms, trusts and savings and loan associations in several states. In most cases, their debt coverage requirements were within the 1.20 to 1.40 range, and 1.25 and 1.30 requirements were the most common.

On the next two pages is a summary of debt coverage factors for six years (24 quarters) in the study of major insurance company commitments cited in the preceding chapters. By and large, these data are consistent with the above comments. In this table, the most frequently occurring figure (mode) is 1.30, and the middle figure (median) is 1.29. Further, if one were to exclude the atypical motel figures, over 9 out of 10 of these average debt coverage factors fall into the 1.20 to 1.40 range.

Debt coverage factors are vitally important to equity investors as well as to mortgage lenders. Their use has much to do with the amount of first mortgage funding typically available for properties.

A knowledge of debt coverage factors can even help professional real estate appraisers in selecting appropriate capitalization rates, as illustrated in Chapter 46.

DEBT COVERAGE FACTORS

As Reflected by Loan Commitments of Major Insurance Companies on Large Income Properties

		Conventional elevator apartments	Conventional nonelevator apartments	Shopping centers (5 or more stores)	Retail stores (less than 5 stores)
1968	IV	1.29	1.30	1.30	1.24
1969	I	1.26	1.29	1.37	1.20
	II	1.39	1.27	1.40	1.32
	III	1.30	1.29	1.31	1.27
	IV	1.39	1.30	1.35	1.26
1970	I	1.31	1.33	1.29	1.29
	II	1.37	1.44	1.41	1.29
	III	1.28	1.31	1.50	1.29
	IV	1.35	1.27	1.38	1.22
1971	I	1.29	1.29	1.36	1.28
	II	1.28	1.26	1.38	1.37
	III	1.26	1.28	1.31	1.32
	IV	1.26	1.30	1.32	1.31
1972	I	1.29	1.29	1.30	1.30
	II	1.28	1.29	1.32	1.10
	III	1.35	1.30	1.32	1.33
	IV	1.30	1.32	1.30	1.50
1973	I	1.28	1.29	1.33	1.40
	II	1.29	1.32	1.37	1.24
	III	1.27	1.31	1.28	1.29
	IV	1.27	1.27	1.24	1.22
1974	I	1.27	1.27	1.34	1.26
	II	1.21	1.31	1.37	1.30
	III	1.45	1.26	1.28	1.25

Source: Ongoing American Life Insurance Association study, "Survey of Mortgage Commitments on Nonresidential Properties Reported by 15 Life Insurance Companies."
Notes: The 15 reporting companies account for over one-half of assets and over one-half of nonfarm mortgages held by all U.S. life insurance companies. Averages in the summary are weighted by number of loans committed. Very few commitments were made for loans on certain property types in certain quarters, and average interest rates were not reported.

Office buildings	Medical office buildings	Commercial warehouses	Industrial warehouses	Manufacturing plants	Motels
1.25	1.33	1.20	1.31	1.21	1.48
1.23		1.17	1.32	1.30	1.56
1.33	1.27	1.23	1.23	1.19	1.57
1.22	1.16	1.30	1.21	1.22	1.51
1.31	1.35	1.34	1.20	1.33	1.55
1.34	1.21	1.26	1.22	1.24	1.95
1.35	1.22	1.23	1.29	1.47	
1.31	1.19	1.44	1.26	1.38	
1.30	1.17		1.36		
1.32	1.35	1.43	1.26	1.31	1.48
1.24	1.28	1.24	1.24	1.25	1.69
1.25	1.25	1.23	1.22	1.25	1.47
1.28	1.32	1.22	1.35	1.30	1.33
1.25	1.36	1.23	1.28	1.54	1.90
1.30	1.34	1.24	1.31	1.43	1.49
1.28	1.28	1.21	1.29	1.27	1.75
1.30	1.34	1.22	1.30	1.27	1.49
1.31	1.31	1.26	1.35	1.30	1.48
1.28	1.26	1.22	1.31	1.24	1.43
1.26	1.25	1.19	1.26	1.32	1.34
1.25	1.24	1.21	1.27	1.33	1.30
1.28	1.21	1.36	1.23	1.29	1.52
1.28	1.34	1.26	1.23	1.24	1.77
1.30	1.43	1.38	1.22	1.26	1.73

 Real property values related to general rate movements

General movements in interest rates do affect the values of income properties but much less than many suppose.

(The following discussion expands on Chapter 37.)

When interest rates change dramatically, one feels a sense of déjà vu; a lot of the same things happen each time. One of them is that professional appraisers and others interested in income properties debate whether capitalization rates (and, conversely, values) follow interest rates closely.

Consider this scenario:

1. Say that, as one step in cooling the economic pace, the Federal Reserve increases the rate charged member banks.

2. So one major bank raises its prime interest rate. Others quickly follow suit.

3. Interest rates on most other forms of short-term borrowings follow suit.

4. So do rates on new long-term borrowings—including bonds and mortgage loans—but the changes here are more moderate.

5. Most large lenders are still interested in making good first mortgage loan investments on income properties, but they naturally expect to get higher yields which parallel those on alternative long-term investments. Their knowledgeable prospective borrowers aren't eager to pay higher interest rates, but their biggest concern is with cash flow. So, the lenders require their higher interest rates but soothe the sting by easing amortizations, thus holding down the mortgage payments. They may also relax their debt coverage and loan-to-value requirements a little.

6. A sizable increase in interest rates has resulted in a limited decrease in cash flow. Some prospective buyers of income properties now want higher yields on their equity investments. The result: Income properties are not quite as attractive now as they would have been with lower rates. However, the diminution in value is much less than proportionate to the increase in interest rates.

To be sure, this is simplistic (clearly, it must be, if we are not to devote a large portion of this book to this one subject), but it will serve our purposes.

One may make these generalizations about rate movements in recent decades:

1. Short-term rates have tended to exhibit a common pattern.

2. Long-term rates have tended to exhibit a common pattern.

3. Short-term rates tend to "drive" long-term rates, but there has been a good deal of "slippage" between the two.

4. Debt service requirements (percent constants) of mortgage loans on major income properties have tended to be much more stable than interest rates.

5. Capitalization rates and values of major income properties appear to parallel typical debt service requirements more closely than they do typical interest rates.

On the next page is a chart showing movements in average rates over a 20-year span. Which of these rates has been the least volatile? The one most closely related to the values of prime major income properties—the percent constants.

22 YEARS OF AVERAGE RATES

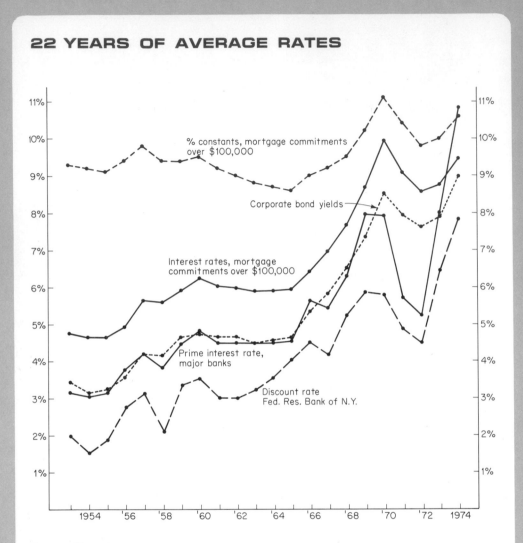

% constants, mortgage commitments over $100,000

Corporate bond yields

Interest rates, mortgage commitments over $100,000

Prime interest rate, major banks

Discount rate Fed. Res. Bank of N.Y.

Sources, Notes:

Terms of Mortgage Loans on Income Properties. The selected terms from data furnished by American Life Insurance Association for new commitments of $100,000 and over each, of selected life insurance companies. The 15 companies account for a little more than one-half of both the total assets and the nonfarm mortgages held by all U.S. life insurance companies. Averages by number of loans. Data on average percent constants (annual level payment to principal and interest, per $100 of debt) limited to cases of full amortization over the loan term and wherein enough data were reported to enable this relationship to be estimated by ALIA. Estimates may not be precise but are believed to be reasonably representative. The figures exclude construction loans, increases in existing loans in a company's portfolio, reapprovals, and loans secured by land only.

Yields on Selected Corporate Bonds. Moody's Investors Service.

Prime Rate, Discount Rate. Annual averages of Federal Reserve data, weighted by number of days.

 **Real estate yields related to the prime rate**

Some rules of thumb attempt to relate overall real estate yields to the prime rate.* They should be treated very skeptically.

One rule occasionally quoted is that yields on prime real properties should be about 1.5 times the prime rate.

Another holds that the yields on prime real properties is typically two or three percentage points higher than the prime rate.

There are others.

To see just how risky such generalizations can be, one need not dig very deeply. As we saw in the preceding chapter, short-term rates (including the prime rate) and long-term rates do not necessarily move in parallel patterns. In 1972 and 1973, the prime rate increased 100 percent. During the same period, yields on investment quality bonds† and the interest rates in new mortgage commitments on prime income properties‡ rose only about 5 percent.

When the prime rate stood at a fraction over 12 percent in mid-1974, were prime income properties typically selling at prices to yield more than 18 percent on the purchase price? No, not even close.

---

* Actually, references to *the* prime rate can be misleading. Beginning in November of 1971, several banks adopted a floating prime rate keyed to money-market variables. Effective in April of 1973, with the adoption of a two-tier or "dual" prime rate, the Federal Reserve began reporting the "large-business prime rate," which is the rate most often published.

† For instance, Moody's average corporate bonds.

‡ Reference: The American Life Insurance Association study cited earlier.

42 Proper capitalization rates and methods

Selection of a proper capitalization rate and capitalization method is critical

Right now, an old income property is producing an annual net operating income of $10,000. Appraiser A looks at the property and decides that:

1. The remaining economic life is 20 years or so.

2. Net operating income is likely to remain just about the same each year and that level annuity treatment is, therefore, acceptable.

3. A speculative interest rate of 10 percent is appropriate.

4. The value remaining in this parcel at the end of the economic life will be nominal.

Appraiser B looks at the same property and makes all of the same assumptions except for one: he believes that net income will decline each year pretty much on a straight-line basis. Well, three out of four isn't bad, right? Wrong! The difference between the two value estimates is more than 25 percent!

An income property has value because it can produce net income for its owner. In the income approach to value, the appraiser translates (capitalizes) the capacity of a property to produce net income for its owner into an estimate of that property's value.

In simplest terms, a capitalization rate is a number which expresses the relationship between a property's anticipated net income (normally, on an annual basis) and that property's value. So:

$$\frac{\text{Net Annual Income}}{\text{Capitalization Rate}} = \text{Value}$$

One can restate this equation so it can be used to see what rates are reflected by actual sales:

$$\frac{\text{Net Annual Income}}{\text{Sale Price}} = \frac{\text{Capitalization Rate}}{\text{Reflected by Sale}}$$

Say an apartment property with a stabilized net operating income of $120,000 per year just sold in an arm's-length transaction for $1,000,000. This sale reflected an overall capitalization rate of ($120,000 ÷ $1,000,000) 12 percent.

Capitalization rates vary from one property to another because of differences in riskiness, in anticipated future changes in net income, and in other factors.

Often (preferably), the appraiser is able to select a single number—an overall rate—which reflects an appropriate rate of return on the investment, any important changes in the level of net operating income that may be expected, and anticipated depreciation or appreciation. If so, the final step in the income approach is very simple; the appraiser simply divides anticipated net income for the typical year in the near future by the appropriate rate which he has selected, as in this example:

$$\frac{\text{Net Income}}{\text{Overall Rate}} = \text{Value}$$

$$\frac{\text{Est. } \$100,000}{\text{Est. } \quad 10.5\%} = \$952,381$$

Rounded less than one-half of 1 percent to $950,000

However, in capitalizing net income, appraisers sometimes select two rates* and employ them in a two-step process. The reason for this is often their belief that (1) land does not depreciate, and (2) improvements do depreciate, so (3) income imputable to these property factors should be treated separately and differently. As they are usually used, most of these "two-step methods" do not parallel what well-Informed investors are doing in the market and are questionable in some other respects.†

Appraisers often testify in courts as experts on what real properties are worth. Usually, there is a sizable difference in their opinions in such cases; otherwise the trials would not ordinarily be held. Large divergencies are often traceable to differences in the selection of the capitalization rates and capitalization methods.

The capitalization process is a sensitive process. Seemingly small differences in rate selection can result in large differences in the value estimate. The professional appraiser needs a thorough understanding of capitalization methods and a thorough understanding of market practices.

---

* An interest rate (or rate of return on the entire investment) and a capitalization rate (an interest rate plus an allowance for depreciation or appreciation).

† See also Chapter 44.

43   Unsound methods, including Built-Up Method

Several methods of selecting capitalization rates are not very sound. One of these is the Built-Up Method or summation method.

This is the Built-Up Method:

1. The appraiser begins with the rate of return on a "safe" investment (often taken as the interest rate on U.S. government bonds which are popularly recognized as being as safe as any long-term investment and can readily be exchanged for cash).

2. To this "safe" rate, the appraiser adds percentage amounts which he believes will compensate for these three disadvantages of investing in the property he is appraising:

   a. The investment in the real property is riskier.

   b. It's also less liquid. Typically, it takes some time to get one's money out of an ownership position in real estate.

   c. Typically, such real estate investments take more of the investors' time and money, while buying, overseeing and selling U.S. government bonds is much less troublesome.

   The sum of these is the interest rate selected (the rate of return to be received on the entire price or value of the property).

	Property A	Property B
"Safe" rate	6.0%	6.0%
Add for additional risk	2.0	3.5
Add for illiquidity	1.0	1.0
Add for investment burden	1.0	1.0
Interest rate selected	10.0%	11.5%

It's easy to see why this is sometimes also called the Summation Method.

3. We have not yet dealt with anticipated depreciation or appreciation in the value of the property. To change an interest rate to a capitalization rate, we must adjust for this factor.

This method of rate selection has serious weaknesses. Several factors are treated individually, even though they are closely interrelated. It is extremely difficult to provide convincing support for individual components—other than the "safe" rate in each case—to the exclusion of some somewhat differing figures. The importance of some of the terms of financing available for the property under appraisement is not reflected directly. There are other shortcomings.

Happily, most professional appraisers have moved on to better methods of rate selection.

 Band of Investment Method

In many cases, appraisers would also do well to shun the Band of Investment Method of selecting capitalization rates.

A popular method of selecting capitalization rates is the Band of Investment Method.

It looks easy. First, the appraiser looks at interest rates required by mortgage lenders and at rates of return being required by the equity investors in properties like the one he's working on. Then he figures the weighted average of these rates based on the loan-to-value ratios of typical mortgages. Finally, he adds an allowance for depreciation. Here's an example:

> You are appraising a shopping center. From a study of the market, you find that mortgage lenders are now willing to approve first mortgage loans up to 75 percent of value with interest at 9 percent, and that equity investors in such projects are typically requiring an 11 percent return on the amount they put in. After checking various guidelines for useful lives (See Chapter 61), you decide that one might reasonably expect the improvements to have a remaining economic life of 50 years. From this point, figuring your rates by the Band of Investment Method will take you only one or two minutes:

Percent of property's total value	×	Rate of return required	=	Weighted factor
Mortgage 75%		9%		6.75%
Equity 25%		11%		2.75
Interest rate selected				9.50%
Allowance for depreciation over 50 years				2.00
Capitalization rate selected				11.50%

It's not hard to understand the popularity of this method of selecting rates. It is quick. It avoids complicated computations. It recognizes that loan-to-value ratios and interest rates on available mortgage loan financing are important to most buyers of income properties. It appears logical and can be described in either simple terms or more impressive terms (". . . a synthesis of representative mortgage and equity yield requirements").

To the extent that what the appraiser does is consistent with what's going on in the market, his work can be soundly supported. Unfortunately, the Band of Investment Method fails this test in most cases. This method assumes that the term of the mortgage loan and size of the payments aren't important to most buyers of income properties. This is patently unrealistic.* It also assumes that the equity investment once made will be held indefinitely and that the typical investor-purchaser isn't vitally concerned with changes over a specific projection period. There are other shortcomings.

When one combines the Band of Investment Method with straight-line treatment† and a residual technique as is so often done, one retreats further away from what is going on in the real world. How many investors approach the purchase of an income property believing that net income will begin to decline at once and decline every year? How many expect that improvements will decline in value every year—and by the same amount each year? How many care a great deal about assigning part of the anticipated net operating income to land and part to improvements? How many don't want to compare the likely yield on an income property investment with alternative forms of investment on a comparable basis?

That appraisers can use the Band of Investment Method when its underlying assumptions don't apply and still develop realistic estimates of value is a tribute to the appraisers' highly developed feeling for property values rather than to the merits of the Band of Investment Method. No doubt Jack Nicklaus could play a respectable round of golf using a 5-iron for every shot, but he—and others—can do much better by selecting the club best suited to each situation.

There are better methods of rate selection, and several of these are discussed in the next two chapters.

---

* For discussions of the great importance attached to sizes of mortgage payments (percent constants) and cash flow, see Chapters 35, 37, and 40.

† Until several years ago, most appraisal students were taught that straight-line treatment was usually preferred if the anticipated net income stream did not possess the characteristics of an annuity.

45 More suitable methods (McLaughlin, Ellwood, Johnson)

Happily, more suitable methods are available to aid the appraiser in selecting appropriate capitalization rates.

1959 was a very good year—for real estate appraising.

In an article published in 1959,* F. J. McLaughlin suggested an improvement in the Band of Investment Method. If mortgage loan amortization is an important factor,† why not weight the mortgage loan constant (reflecting both interest and amortization) instead of weighting just the mortgage loan interest rate?

Also in 1959, L. W. Ellwood published a book‡ which was to have tremendous impact on the appraisal field. In addition to recognizing the importance of loan-to-value ratios, of mortgage loan interest rates, of required yields on equity (as does the Band of Investment Method), and of loan amortization (as in the improvement suggested by F. J. McLaughlin), the Ellwood book of precomputed rates allowed for recognition of other important facts of life. Don't well-informed prospective buyers of major income properties usually make projections for a limited number of years? Aren't they interested in the potential increase or decrease in the equity position because of principal reduction and because of appreciation or depreciation? Well then, why not set up tables of capitalization rate factors which can reflect such interests? By the 1970s, the Ellwood Method had become widely recognized as one of the most important methods available to professional appraisers to aid them in selecting appropriate capitalization rates.§

In 1972, a book of totally precomputed overall rates by I. E. Johnson¶ was published. Essentially similar to L. W. Ellwood's work, I. E. Johnson's presentation may be more readily grasped by some.

Clearly, these mortgage-equity techniques have some important advantages, but they are not necessarily the "treatment of choice" in every case. Some of the most

---

* Frank J. McLaughlin, "Proper Capitalization Rates." *The Appraisal Journal,* October, 1959, 27: 543–547.

† And it is; see Chapter 37.

‡ L. W. Ellwood, *Ellwood Tables for Real Estate Appraising and Financing,* 1959, published by the author. (In 1967, the American Institute of Real Estate Appraisers published the second edition of Mr. Ellwood's book. In 1970, AIREA published the third edition, this in two parts.)

§ Ellwood factors are also useful in market analysis and real estate counseling. For example, one can readily figure the impact on equity yield of varying assumptions about appreciation or depreciation of a particular income property investment under consideration. As another example, one can use Ellwood factors to make adjustments in prices of comparable sales to reflect important differences in terms of financing.

¶ Irvin E. Johnson, *The Instant Mortgage-Equity Technique,* D. C. Heath and Company, Lexington, Mass., 1972.

sophisticated and able appraisers feel uneasy about the possibility of overanalysis at times. A sale of a shopping center property may reflect an overall rate of 10.7 percent which the informed appraiser or analyst knows to reflect a combination of several factors. Whether that 10.7 percent rate can realistically and reliably be broken down into factors imputable to various components is a decision which must be made, largely on the basis of the quantity and quality of the information which the appraiser or analyst has to work with in each particular case.

Several of the best-known methods of selecting capitalization rates have been mentioned in this book. Some others have not. The point is not to find one method which is always best and therefore should be used in every case. Not at all. Instead, there are three points that should be made:

1. Some methods of selecting capitalization rates have serious limitations or defects. These methods should be shunned in most cases.

2. Assumptions about how income flow and other rewards of property ownership will be received can vary from one appraisal to another. Assumptions implicit in selecting and using captialization rates vary from one method to another.

3. Most professional appraisers do not feel "married" to one particular method. Rather, they recognize the value of understanding tho variety of tools that are available and selecting the one tool which is most appropriate for each job.

The next chapter explains a method of rate selection which can be very useful but is not widely known.

46 Gettel's Method

The Gettel Method: Here is a quick method of selecting capitalization rates which works well in some cases.

Wouldn't it be nice if there were a valid method of selecting capitalization rates which took typical mortgage loan terms into account but didn't involve either complicated arithmetic or tables? Well, there is one.

From earlier sections, we already know that typical mortgage loan-to-value ratios, percent constants, and debt coverage factors are of keen interest to well-informed investors in major income properties. Select the three figures most representative for the property under consideration and multiply them together for a capitalization rate.

Example:

Assume that you are appraising a modern apartment project. From analysis of sales and in-depth interviews, you learn that the most typical new long-term financing for the subject property right now would involve:

a. a first mortgage loan equivalent to 80 percent of value,

b. level payments to principal and interest based on an 11.0 percent constant (i.e., payments each year equal to 11 percent of the original amount borrowed), and

c. a debt coverage factor of 1.30 (i.e., projected net operating income is 30 percent higher than payments to principal and interest).

Your selected capitalization rate: 80% × 11% × 1.30 = 11.4%.

This is an overall rate. Its use is quite simple and direct. If the subject apartment project is likely to produce a net income (before deductions for debt service and depreciation) of $100,000 in the typical year in the near future, then the value of this property may be estimated at ($100,000 ÷ 0.114 = $877,193, rounded less than one-half of 1 percent) $880,000.

If this method is to be used well, one must have a thorough understanding of mortgage lending practices, but this is also true of other acceptable mortgage-equity methods of selecting appropriate capitalizarion rates. If one is to use the tables prepared by L. W. Ellwood or I. E. Johnson, one must already have found out the most appropriate loan-to-value ratio, most appropriate loan interest rate, and the most appropriate amortization. In the Gettel Method, one simply employs a third financing term in lieu of certain factors (return on equity and appreciation or depreciation during the projection period) employed in these widely used mortgage-equity methods. Not treating some of these other items individually can be an advantage or a disadvantage depending upon the quantity and quality of the data available to the appraiser. If the appraiser has credible data available on debt coverage factors, but lacks convincing data on which to project likely appreciation or depreciation during a projection period, he might feel justified in opting for this simpler method.

Perhaps the most frequent use for this method will be to provide a quick check on the reasonableness of overall capitalization rates as selected by the more detailed methods.

On the next page is a table showing the relationship of three mortgage loan factors to overall capitalization rates. This is by way of illustration only. One of the advantages of this method is that no tables at all are needed; once the reader understands the method and selects the most typical loan factors for the property under appraisement, an overall capitalization rate can be worked out faster than it can be looked up in a set of tables.

DEVELOPMENT OF THE BASIC EQUATION OF THE GETTEL METHOD

(For Algebra Buffs Only)

1. Begin with *the* classic value equation:

$$\frac{\text{Income}}{\text{Cap. Rate}} = \text{Value}$$

2. Take note that, by definition of the terms involved, these three equations are valid:

   a. $\text{Income} = (\text{Debt Coverage Factor}) (\text{Debt Service \$})$

   b. $\text{Value} = \dfrac{\text{Mortgage Loan Amount}}{\text{Mortgage Loan \%}}$

   c. $\text{Mortgage Loan Amount} = \dfrac{\text{Debt Service \$}}{\text{\% Constant}}$

3. Then, by substitution, we have: $(\text{Debt Service \$}) (\text{Debt Cov. Factor}) = \dfrac{\text{Mortgage Loan Amt.}}{\text{Mortgage Loan \%}}$

4. Cross multiply: $(\text{Cap. Rate}) (\text{Mortgage Loan Amt.}) = (\text{Debt Service \$}) (\text{Mortgage Loan \%}) (\text{Debt. Cov. Factor})$

5. And substitute again: $(\text{Cap. Rate}) \dfrac{(\text{Debt Service \$})}{\text{\% Constant}} = (\text{Debt Service \$}) (\text{Mortgage Loan \%}) (\text{Debt. Cov. Factor})$

6. Multiply both sides by (% Constant): $(\text{Cap. Rate}) (\text{Debt Service \$}) = (\text{Debt Service \$}) (\text{Mortgage Loan \%}) (\text{Debt. Cov. Factor}) (\text{\% Constant})$

7. And divide by (Debt Service \$): $\text{Cap. Rate} = (\text{Mortgage Loan \%}) (\text{Debt. Cov. Factor}) (\text{\% Constant})$

EXAMPLES OF RATE SELECTION
BY THE GETTEL METHOD

Loan-to-value %	Percent constant	Debt coverage factor	Overall capitalization rate
66$^2/_3$%	11.0%	1.20	8.80%
		1.30	9.53
		1.50	11.00
	12.0%	1.20	9.60%
		1.30	10.40
		1.50	12.00
	13.0%	1.20	10.40%
		1.30	11.27
		1.50	13.00
75%	10.0%	1.20	9.00%
		1.30	9.75
		1.50	11.25
	11.0%	1.20	9.90%
		1.30	10.73
		1.50	12.38
	12.0%	1.20	10.80%
		1.30	11.70
		1.50	13.50
85%	9.0%	1.10	8.42%
		1.20	9.18
		1.30	9.95
	10.0%	1.10	9.35%
		1.20	10.20
		1.30	11.05
	11.0%	1.10	10.29%
		1.20	11.22
		1.30	12.16

 How long a mortgage loan term
is acceptable to lenders—I

**Some lenders have adopted this guideline for loans on shopping centers
and other properties when guaranteed income from major tenants is of
primary importance: The loan term should not exceed the primary term
of the major tenant by more than five years. (If more than one major
tenant is involved in one property, a weighted average of their primary
terms may be added to five years.)**

The suitability of this guideline can vary from case to case.

In making large, long-term loans on some tenant-occupied properties—
particularly new shopping centers and office buildings—lenders often follow this
pattern:

   a. Rental income from major (highly rated) tenants should be adequate to
      cover debt service (principal and interest payments).

   b. Additional income (primarily, guaranteed rent from other tenants) should
      be sufficient to cover likely expenses and to provide a "cushion."*

   c. The term of the loan should not extend more than a reasonable period—
      often taken as five years—beyond the primary terms of the major tenants.

A hypothetical but fairly representative example is set out on the next two pages.

Wise mortgage loan underwriters appreciate the value of time-tested guidelines,
but they know that quality factors vary greatly from one case to another. In one instance, a lender may want no loan balance outstanding beyond the primary terms
of "blue chip" tenants because of questionable location factors. In another instance, property factors and location factors may be so strong that a substantially
longer term appears justified.

The point is this: If the loan term extends beyond the primary terms of "bullet-
proof" leases, then the lender must look to other factors for security for the unpaid
balance . . . and *that* leads us right into the discussion in the next chapter.

* For a discussion of debt coverage factors, see Chapter 39.

SUMMARY OF MORTGAGE LOAN OFFERING

Proposed Seaview Shopping Center, San Mateo County, California

PRINCIPAL TERMS OF PROPOSED MORTGAGE LOAN:

Amount:	$1,000,000
Interest Rate:	9%
Annual Constant:	10.75% (level monthly amortization over 20 years and 3 months)

SUMMARY OF SELECTED LEASE TERMS:

No.	Type of tenant	Rating	Gross leasable area (sq. ft.)	Guaranteed minimum:			Lease term:	
				Total	(Per sq. ft.)	%	Primary (yrs.)	Options
1	Supermarket	Major	17,500	$ 43,750	($2.50)	1.5	20 Yrs.	3 @ 5
2	Restaurant	Major	2,500	15,000	($6.00)	7	10	
3	Jr. Dept.	Local	10,000	25,000	($2.50)	3	20	2 @ 5
4	Variety	Major	10,000	26,500	($2.65)	4	15	5 @ 5
5	Ladies' Wear	Major	2,000	7,000	($3.50)	5	10	1 @ 5
6	Hardware	Local	5,000	11,250	($2.25)	4	10	3 @ 5
7	Drugs	Major	7,500	22,500	($3.00)	3	15	2 @ 5
8	Beauty Shop	Local	1,000	5,000	($5.00)	8	5	
9	Cleaners	Local	1,500	7,500	($5.00)	8	5	
10–16	Others	Local	12,000	58,000	(Var.)	Var.	5	
All			69,000 Sq. Ft.	$221,500				

MORTGAGE LOAN ANALYST'S COMMENTS:

1. Developer is well regarded, but has limited financial capacity.

2. Proposed loan amount is a little less than 75 percent of the independent appraisal (see enclosed report), which appears well supported.

3. We can look to guaranteed minimum income from strong tenants ($114,750) to cover debt service (10.75% of $1,000,000 = $107,500).

4. Anticipated minimum rents from other tenants appear adequate to meet expenses (see attached summary of projected expenses and required tenant contributions) and provide a safe margin.

5. The composite term of the major tenants was computed as follows:

No. 1	20 years @	$ 43,750	=	$ 875,000
No. 2	10 years @	15,000	=	150,000
No. 4	15 years @	26,500	=	397,500
No. 5	10 years @	7,000	=	70,000
No. 7	15 years @	22,500	=	337,500
		$114,750		$1,830,000

Dollar-weighted average ($1,830,000 ÷ $114,750): 15.95 years. The proposed term (20.25 years) is less than 5 years longer than this. In view of several important quality attributes in this case—most notably the strong and improving trading area—this exposure appears acceptable.

6. Approval recommended.

How long a mortgage loan term is acceptable to lenders?

One of the factors they consider is the loan balance at a particular time in the future.

If you apply for a mortgage loan, several factors are likely to have a bearing on the maximum term available to you:

1. Custom

2. Lease terms

3. Type of real estate

4. Age, condition, and design of real estate

5. Location factors

6. Competition

As seen in earlier chapters, there are often pressures on mortgage loan officers to stretch out the loan terms. And often these mortgage loan officers must deal with situations like these:

1. A blue-chip tenant is bound by lease to occupy a property for the next 20 years, and this tenant's rent will cover operating expenses and loan payments safely. However, we can't be sure this tenant will exercise its renewal option and remain here after the 20-year primary term. Say the lender approves a loan with an 8 percent interest rate and a 9.0 percent annual constant* (level monthly payments over 27 years, 7 months). What percentage of the loan amount will remain unpaid after the "safe" 20-year period? (Answer: Approximately 51 percent of the loan amount will still be outstanding if there were no prepayments.)

2. For the sake of another example, suppose that Lender A has been committing on loans on new garden apartments with payments based on a 10 percent constant (with an interest rate of 9 percent and with level payments for 25 years and 8 months). Recently, other lenders have begun offering loan commitments on the basis of a 9.5 percent annual constant (with the same interest rate of 9 percent but with a term of 32 years and 10 months). Lender A is considering meeting this competition. Even though most of its loans are prepaid in 10 or 15 years, Lender A is curious

---

* For a discussion of mortgage loan constants, see Chapter 37.

about this: what is the potential increase in exposure? (Answer: This longer term may well be justified, but it is interesting to note that lowering the annual constant just one-half of 1 percent here would mean that, while the entire loan amount had to be paid in 25 years and 8 months before, now up to 50 percent of the loan amount still may be outstanding at the end of this period.)

3. Let's say a bank wants to make a loan on a new motel. The bank has agreed with the borrower on an interest rate of 9 percent. It has also agreed to debt service (principal and interest payments) based on a 12.0 percent constant, which would give full amortization in 18 years, but the bank doesn't want its money "out" on this property that long, so it commits for 10 years, with the principal balance outstanding at the end of 10 years to be repaid in one "balloon" payment. How large is the "balloon"? (Answer: Assuming no prepayments during the 10-year term, approximately 65.9 percent of the original principal amount will still be unpaid.)

On the following pages are selected figures* which can be used for computations of this sort.

---

* Should they be desired by the reader, more complete tables may be purchased from the American Institute of Real Estate Appraisers, Financial Publishing Company, and others.

PERCENT OF LOAN UNPAID AFTER A GIVEN NUMBER OF YEARS

(Assumptions: Level Monthly Payments Based on Full Amortization during Term of Loan. No Prepayments. No Delinquent Payments.)

Original loan term (years)	Elapsed time (years)	6%	6½%	7%	7½%	8%
10	5	57.4	58.0	58.6	59.2	59.8
	10					
	15					
	20					
	25					
	30					
15	5	76.0	76.7	77.4	78.1	78.8
	10	43.6	44.5	45.4	46.3	47.1
	15					
	20					
	25					
	30					
20	5	84.9	85.6	86.3	86.9	87.5
	10	64.5	65.7	66.8	67.9	68.9
	15	37.1	38.1	39.2	40.2	41.3
	20					
	25					
	30					
25	5	89.9	90.6	91.2	91.7	92.3
	10	76.4	77.5	78.6	79.7	80.8
	15	58.0	59.5	60.9	62.3	63.6
	20	33.3	34.5	35.7	36.9	38.1
	25					
	30					
30	5	93.1	93.6	94.1	94.6	95.1
	10	83.7	84.8	85.8	86.8	87.7
	15	71.0	72.6	74.0	75.4	76.8
	20	54.0	55.7	57.3	58.9	60.5
	25	31.0	32.3	33.6	34.9	36.2
	30					
40	5	96.5	96.9	97.3	97.6	97.9
	10	91.8	92.6	93.8	94.1	94.8
	15	85.4	86.7	87.9	89.0	90.1
	20	76.8	78.5	80.2	81.7	83.1
	25	65.2	67.2	69.1	71.0	72.8
	30	49.6	51.6	53.5	55.4	57.3

Example: A $100,000 loan called for 9 percent interest and full amortization via level monthly payments over 30 years. Assuming that payments are made when due (no pre-

8¹/₂%	9%	9¹/₂%	10%	10¹/₂%	11%	12%	15%
60.4	61.0	61.6	62.2	62.8	63.4	64.5	67.8
79.4	80.1	80.7	81.3	81.9	82.5	83.7	86.8
48.0	48.9	49.7	50.6	51.4	52.3	54.0	58.8
88.1	88.7	89.3	89.8	90.3	90.8	91.7	94.1
70.0	71.0	72.0	73.0	74.0	74.9	76.7	81.6
42.3	43.3	44.4	45.4	46.4	47.5	49.5	55.4
92.8	93.3	93.7	94.2	94.6	95.0	95.7	97.3
81.8	82.7	83.7	84.6	85.4	86.2	87.8	91.5
64.9	66.2	67.5	68.8	70.0	71.2	73.4	79.4
39.2	40.4	41.6	42.8	43.9	45.1	47.3	53.8
95.5	95.9	96.2	96.6	96.9	97.2	97.7	98.7
88.6	89.4	90.2	90.9	91.6	92.3	93.4	96.0
78.1	79.3	80.5	81.7	82.8	83.8	85.7	90.3
62.0	63.5	65.0	66.4	67.8	69.1	71.7	78.4
37.5	38.8	40.0	41.3	42.6	43.8	46.2	53.1
98.2	98.4	98.6	98.8	98.9	99.1	99.3	99.7
95.3	95.9	96.3	96.8	97.1	97.5	98.0	99.1
91.0	91.9	92.7	93.4	94.1	94.7	95.8	97.8
84.5	85.7	86.9	88.0	89.0	89.9	91.6	95.2
74.4	76.1	77.6	79.0	80.4	81.7	84.0	89.5
59.1	60.9	62.6	64.3	65.8	67.4	70.3	77.7

payments), what will the principal balance be at the end of 10 years? Answer: (approximately 89.4% of $100,000) approximately $89,400.

49

Formula for maximum rent for "blue chip" tenants

"Blue chip" chain store operators know how important their leases are to developers. Some of them use this formula to decide the maximum guaranteed rent they will pay for a store: Likely dollar cost (or value) of store × the typical mortgage loan constant.[*]

Perhaps this can best be illustrated by a modern parable:

Developer has optioned a 6-acre tract and wants to build a neighborhood shopping center. Developer knows that if one strong "magnet" will lease space here, attracting other tenants will be easier, and the project will have more appeal to mortgage lenders.

Highly rated Chain Store is considering an 18,500-square-foot store here, which, with a portion of the site and site improvements, would typically cost $400,000. Well-informed Chain Store knows that the typical mortgage loan constant for such projects now is 10 percent, and Chain Store offers to pay rent of (10 percent of $400,000) $40,000 per year.

In addition, Chain Store offers to pay its pro rata share of property expenses, so that this would be a net lease. Chain Store would also agree to a typical percentage (or overage) rent clause, which would result in additional rent if its sales in this store proved to be very strong.

With this arrangement, all the rent would go to debt service; there would be no cash flow, and—as discussed earlier[†]—cash flow in the near term is the reward many investors value most.

Developer asks for higher rent. Chain Store refuses. No stranger to developing store properties, Chain Store knows that (1) once it or another "magnet" is signed, Developer can proceed to lease to others at higher rental rates; and that (2) if Developer refuses, Chain Store—given its financial capacity and reputation—can probably make a similar agreement with another developer or develop a property itself ("mortgaging out" on the cost of its own store, making payments to debt service based on a 10 percent constant instead of paying rent to someone else in the same amount, and enjoying rewards of a developer as well as the risks and headaches of a developer).

Developer finds no better alternative, knows that successful developing is often a matter of the "art of the possible," and agrees to these terms. From the lease agreement with Chain Store, Developer didn't gain any cash flow, but

[*] For a discussion of mortgage loan constants, see Chapter 37.

[†] See Chapter 35.

Developer did gain several benefits: a strong "magnet" to draw traffic for the rest of the center plus a contractor's profit, mortgage amortization, and possible appreciation from Chain Store's portion.

Developer leased the balance of the center well and built it. Developer prospered.

So did Chain Store.

No tenant wants to pay more than it has to to get a good location. In the case of very strong chains which can borrow 100 percent of the cost of developing a property ("mortgage out"), doing so and paying debt service (constant $\times$ the mortgage amount) is an alternative to paying higher rent to a developer. Thus, the typical constant is taken by some of these very strong chains as the maximum rent they will agree to pay someone else to provide a store.

**It appears that typical operating ratios for apartment buildings in the
United States and Canada have changed relatively little in recent years.**

The 1970s have brought many changes in the apartment field: dramatic increases
in the number of units, some changes in design, large increases in the dollar
amounts of both rents and expenses, and thoughts of shifting more of the expense
burden (particularly for utilities) to tenants.

However, in *percentage* terms, operating figures have been relatively stable.

At least that appears to be a reasonable *generalization* from a review of annual
experience reports published by the Institute of Real Estate Management of the National Association of Realtors.

On the next page is a summary of typical operating percentages for over a quarter
of a million apartment units, which figures were drawn from the 1974 edition of
IREM's *Income/Expense Analysis.*

Of more help in spotting trends in operating ratios are those data in one section of
IREM's report which compare operating results from year to year in the same 283
buildings.* One the last page of this chapter is a summary of these comparative
data. A reasonable generalization: While the percentage of net operating income
may vary widely from one property type to another (e.g., one age group to another),
this percentage may vary little from year to year *for the same or very closely comparable buildings.*

IREM's reports provide very useful averages against which one may weigh (actual
past or likely future) operating figures in one particular apartment project. However, in using these data to analyze a particular property, the real estate professional must be alert to those specific local conditions and those individual property
factors likely to account for differences—perhaps large differences—in operating
results for that particular property.

---

* In looking for trends over time, a consistent sample is likely to be more reliable than much larger samples
which vary from year to year. This is not to say that this consistent sample is very small; these 283 buildings
house over 40,000 U.S. and Canadian apartments.

TYPICAL OPERATING RATIOS FOR UNFURNISHED APARTMENTS

	Elevator buildings	Low-rise 12–24 units	Low-rise 25 units and over	Garden-type buildings
Gross Possible Total Income	100.0%	100.0%	100.0%	100.0%
(Vacancies and Delinquents)	(3.1)	(4.8)	(5.4)	(6.1)
(Maintenance and Operating)	(19.3)	(17.5)	(16.9)	(16.8)
(Utilities)	(10.1)	(11.4)	(9.7)	(11.0)
(Management and Administrative)	(6.0)	(7.4)	(6.8)	(7.2)
(Taxes and Insurance)	(17.7)	(19.2)	(17.1)	(13.9)
Net Operating Income before Replacements and Depreciation	45.3%	45.4%	48.2%	47.3%
Size of Sample:				
Number of Buildings	395	344	444	1,066
Number of Apartments	66,414	6,689	30,438	165,101
Number of Rooms	237,076	25,178	120,034	659,581

Note: The above percentages are based upon the number of rooms reporting each particular item. Percentages, therefore, do not total exactly 100%.

Source: These 1973 operating percentages were abstracted from the 1974 edition of *Income/Expense Analysis* by permission from the publisher, the Institute of Real Estate Management, 155 East Superior Street, Chicago, Ill. 60611.

COMPARISON OF OPERATING RESULTS FROM YEAR TO YEAR IN THE SAME 283 BUILDINGS

Type of buildings (number in sample)	Year	Net operating income as % of gross possible total income
Unfurnished Elevator Buildings Built 1946–1960	1970	47.5%
	1971	47.5
(25 buildings)	1972	44.4
	1973	44.1
Unfurnished Elevator Buildings Built 1961–1967	1970	53.3%
	1971	49.8
(34 buildings)	1972	49.2
	1973	47.9
Unfurnished, Low-Rise, 12–24 Units, Built 1921–1930	1970	34.5%
	1971	33.7
(22 buildings)	1972	35.1
	1973	37.0
Unfurnished, Low-Rise, 12–24 Units, Built 1961–1970	1970	50.6%
	1971	50.9
(18 buildings)	1972	50.8
	1973	48.7
Unfurnished, Low-Rise, 25 Units and Over, Built 1921–1930	1970	38.3%
	1971	34.0
(29 buildings)	1972	36.0
	1973	37.3
Unfurnished, Low-Rise, 25 Units and Over, Built 1961–1967	1970	49.5%
	1971	48.4
(10 buildings)	1972	45.2
	1973	48.7
Unfurnished Garden Apartments Built 1946–1960	1970	45.8%
	1971	46.9
(41 buildings)	1972	46.7
	1973	43.0
Unfurnished Garden Apartments Built 1961–1967	1970	53.2%
	1971	52.1
(104 buildings)	1972	51.4
	1973	51.4

Source: Figures abstracted by permission from the 1974 Edition of *Income/Expense Analysis* published by the Institute of Real Estate Management, 155 East Superior Street, Chicago, Ill. 60611.

Both operating expenses and rents in major office buildings have risen dramatically in recent years.

However, the typical relationship between the two—the operating ratio—has changed much less.

The outstanding source of operating data on office buildings in North America is the *Office Building Experience Exchange Report.**

The 1974 version sampled 1973 operations of 676 office buildings in 88 cities in the United States and Canada. This sampling included over 145 million square feet of rentable area. On a total-sample basis, operating expenses† claimed 79.8 percent of the operating income received. Management expenses (total operating expenses less fixed charges such as real estate taxes and insurance) ran 43.2 percent of the operating income. Here is a graphic representation of certain expense percentages from the report:

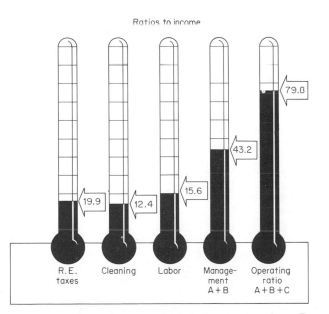

Source: Directly reprinted from the *Office Building Experience Exchange Report* for the calendar year 1973.

* This report has been published annually since 1922 by the Building Owners and Managers Association International, 224 South Michigan Avenue, Chicago, Ill. 60604.

† Not included in operating expenses were capital costs or financial costs such as ground rent, interest, and income taxes.

Over the years, the dollar amounts of both rents and expenses have been marching rather steadily and strongly upward. The average rent per square foot in the 1974 report was over 43 percent higher than the corresponding figure in the 1964 report. Expense figures increased sharply over this 10-year period too.

While the dollar amounts have changed radically in recent decades, the operating ratios or percentages have not. The so-called management expenses* have even declined a little as a percentage of operating income in recent decades.

Source: Directly reprinted from the *Office Building Experience Exchange Report* for the calendar year 1973.

Useful and interesting though it may be, knowledge of such general income-to-expense ratios for major office buildings will not take the place of individual analysis in a specific case. There is not one amorphous market for office space; rather, there are a great number of submarkets. Within individual submarkets, there are often several types or classes of office space.

Expense ratios can vary widely with differences in several factors. If one is studying a particular (proposed or existing) office building, the most useful data in any operating experience report are likely to be those separated by age of building, by height, by size, by size of city, by region, by specific city, and by other factors. In short, one does not want to compare operations of a tall, new building in San Francisco with those of a short, old building in a quiet village.

An important caveat: Data from operating experience reports can be very helpful to real estate professionals, but should not be relied on without analysis of specific local data. Is the construction of this particular building such that maintenance—or utility costs or insurance rates—will be higher or lower than usual? What is the (actual or likely) real estate tax burden on this building? What is the insurance rating? What are the trends in this particular submarket?

* Operating expenses other than fixed charges such as real estate taxes, insurance, and depreciation.

 Typical operating percentages for shopping centers

Much the same thing can be said about shopping centers.

While markedly changed in dollar amounts, typical operations remained surprisingly steady in percentage terms in recent years.

Typical operating percentages found in hundreds of shopping centers are summarized on the next three pages.

Two Urban Land Institute studies made three years apart showed dramatic change in dollar amounts but little change in percentage amounts. For example, the typical (median) operating balance in regional centers rose by a whopping 85 percent in *dollar amounts* but stayed at an almost identical level *as a percentage* of income.

TYPICAL OPERATING PERCENTAGES FOR NEIGHBORHOOD SHOPPING CENTERS*

	Median % in 1972 study (124 centers)	Median % in 1975 study (163 centers)
OPERATING RECEIPTS:		
Rent	95.5%	94.4%
Common area charges	3.6	3.7
Other charges	2.5	3.7
Total Operating Receipts	100.0%	100.0%
OPERATING EXPENSES:		
Total maintenance and housekeeping expenses	8.0%	6.8%
Advertising and promotion	1.0	0.7
Real estate taxes	13.3	12.2
Insurance	2.0	2.0
General and administrative	5.4	4.9
Total Operating Expenses	30.0%	28.4%
OPERATING BALANCE	70.0%	71.6%

Note: Because these percentages are medians, detail figures do not add to totals.

* The neighborhood shopping center provides "convenience" goods such as food, drugs, and personal services. The supermarket is usually the principal tenant in the neighborhood shopping center. Typical size: 25,000–100,000 square feet of gross leasable area.

From: 1972 and 1975 Editions of *Dollars and Cents of Shopping Centers,* reprinted with permission of ULI—the Urban Land Institute, 1200 18th Street, N.W., Washington, D.C. 20036.

TYPICAL OPERATING PERCENTAGES FOR COMMUNITY SHOPPING CENTERS*

	Median % in 1972 study (120 centers)	Median % in 1975 study (170 centers)
OPERATING RECEIPTS:		
Rent	96.1%	95.1%
Common area charges	3.2	3.4
Other charges	3.0	2.6
Total Operating Receipts	100.0%	100.0%
OPERATING EXPENSES:		
Total maintenance and housekeeping expenses	9.0%	8.9%
Advertising and promotion	1.3	0.9
Real estate taxes	12.1	12.3
Insurance	2.0	1.8
General and administrative	5.5	5.2
Total Operating Expenses	34.0%	31.4%
OPERATING BALANCE	66.0%	68.5%

Note: Because these percentages are medians, detail figures do not add to totals.

* The community center provides "convenience goods" plus a range of "shopping goods" as well. A junior department store or a variety store is the principal tenant of the community center. Typical size: 80,000–270,000 square feet of gross leasable area.

From: 1972 and 1975 Editions of *Dollars and Cents of Shopping Centers,* reprinted with permission of ULI—the Urban Land Institute, 1200 18th Street, N.W., Washington, D.C. 20036.

TYPICAL OPERATING PERCENTAGES FOR REGIONAL SHOPPING CENTERS*

	Median % in 1972 study (109 centers)	Median % in 1975 study (109 centers)
OPERATING RECEIPTS:		
Rent	88.1%	86.1%
Common area charges	7.5	8.1
Other charges	4.8	3.9
Total Operating Receipts	100.0%	100.0%
OPERATING EXPENSES:		
Total maintenance and housekeeping expenses	12.6%	14.1%
Advertising and promotion	1.5	1.2
Real estate taxes	12.0	11.1
Insurance	1.2	1.2
General and administrative	5.2	5.0
Total Operating Expenses	34.8%	34.5%
OPERATING BALANCE	65.2%	65.4%

Note: Because these percentages are medians, detail figures do not add to totals.

* The regional shopping center provides a variety and depth of "shopping goods" comparable to a central business district of a small city. One or more major or full-line department stores are the principal tenants. Typical size: 300,000–850,000 square feet of gross leasable area.

From: 1972 and 1975 Editions of *Dollars and Cents of Shopping Centers,* reprinted with permission of ULI—the Urban Land Institute, 1200 18th Street, N.W., Washington, D.C. 20036.

53 Typical operating percentages for motels

Similarly, typical operating ratios for motels have been surprisingly steady over the past several years.

Each year since 1938, *Motel/Motor Inn Journal* has carried out a fascinating and enlightening survey of motel operations across the continental United States. In the 11-year summary on page 160, note how little most of the operating costs have changed from year to year as a percentage of room sales.

Operating ratios varied from small motels to large motels, as shown on page 162. This is partly because operations are simpler in small motels, and owners handle more of the work themselves.

One must keep in mind that these are *average* figures. They were based upon large samples—samples which included large and small, new and old, north and south, efficient and inefficient, profitable and unprofitable. Individual variations can be sizable. Though interesting and useful, these averages will not take the place of thorough, individual analysis in a specific case.

SCHEDULE OF EXPENSES AND NET PROFITS FROM ROOM SALES ONLY*

	1974	1973	1972	1971
Room sales	100.00%	100.00%	100.00%	100.00%
Operating expenses:				
Salaries and wages	22.46%	22.04%	24.49%	24.43%
Executive salaries	3.56%	2.55%	3.97%	3.60%
Laundry	2.19%	4.32%	2.78%	3.14%
Linen and china replacement	2.02%	1.38%	1.34%	1.47%
Cleaning and other supplies	3.13%	3.72%	2.92%	3.11%
Printing, stationery, and advertising	5.11%	4.10%	3.56%	4.14%
Telephone, telegraph, and postage	3.10%	2.73%	2.44%	2.70%
Utilities	7.06%	6.50%	5.60%	5.55%
Repairs	6.15%	4.52%	4.77%	3.84%
Other expenses	4.73%	6.21%	6.27%	6.54%
TOTAL OPERATING EXPENSES	59.51%	58.08%	58.14%	58.52%
Capital expenses:				
Taxes	4.95%	5.07%	5.31%	5.95%
Insurance	2.36%	2.02%	2.22%	2.08%
Rent	2.42%	2.18%	5.81%	4.44%
Interest	9.87%	10.42%	8.29%	9.78%
Depreciation and amortization	15.31%	15.31%	12.66%	14.17%
TOTAL CAPITAL EXPENSES	34.91%	35.00%	34.29%	36.42%
TOTAL EXPENSES	94.42%	93.08%	92.43%	94.94%
NET PROFIT ON ROOM SALES	5.58%	6.92%	7.57%	5.06%

* Copyright July 1975 issue of *Motel/Motor Inn Journal,* Temple, Texas. Further reproduction in part or in whole prohibited unless written permission obtained from the copyright owner.

1970	1969	1968	1967	1966	1965	1964
100.00%	100.00%	100.00%	100.00%	100.00%	100.00%	100.00%
23.87%	22.41%	20.27%	20.88%	20.87%	20.56%	18.45%
3.44%	3.46%	4.41%	4.10%	4.05%	4.61%	3.78%
2.35%	3.16%	3.22%	3.98%	3.92%	3.59%	3.58%
1.40%	1.10%	1.34%	1.22%	1.27%	1.54%	1.70%
2.49%	2.92%	3.06%	2.73%	2.88%	2.97%	2.68%
4.16%	3.54%	3.86%	4.34%	3.60%	3.97%	4.50%
2.22%	2.35%	2.52%	2.53%	2.58%	2.06%	1.88%
5.23%	5.61%	5.51%	5.30%	5.96%	5.76%	5.79%
3.90%	4.17%	4.47%	4.88%	4.38%	4.29%	4.27%
8.67%	8.91%	8.63%	8.58%	8.08%	8.26%	6.63%
57.73%	57.63%	57.29%	58.54%	57.59%	57.61%	53.35%
5.25%	4.32%	4.83%	4.72%	4.58%	4.46%	4.33%
1.77%	1.85%	1.76%	1.46%	1.81%	1.60%	1.48%
4.42%	4.79%	4.86%	7.64%	5.49%	6.56%	10.73%
9.19%	9.41%	8.32%	7.57%	9.31%	8.29%	7.55%
14.41%	15.94%	15.02%	13.24%	13.65%	13.72%	13.98%
35.04%	36.31%	34.79%	34.63%	34.84%	34.63%	38.07%
92.77%	93.94%	92.08%	93.17%	92.43%	92.24%	91.42%
7.23%	6.06%	7.92%	6.83%	7.57%	7.76%	8.58%

1974 OPERATIONS BY SIZE OF MOTEL

	20 Units and under	61–100 Units	126 Units and over
Income:			
Room rentals	94.78%	76.32%	73.95%
Food service	2.24%	15.50%	17.29%
Sundry sales	.67%	.82%	4.60%
Rents, concessions, etc.	1.03%	3.73%	1.81%
Other Income	1.28%	3.63%	2.35%
TOTAL INCOME	100.00%	100.00%	100.00%
Operating expenses:			
Salaries and wages	9.01%	22.56%	27.91%
Executive salaries	1.91%	4.52%	4.73%
Laundry	2.34%	.94%	2.04%
Linen, chinaware, glassware	2.07%	1.26%	1.85%
Advertising, printing, stationery	2.07%	3.18%	5.72%
Payroll, Taxes, insurance	.92%	2.23%	2.05%
Heat, light, and power	8.94%	4.79%	4.45%
Repairs and maintenance	4.16%	4.91%	5.39%
Cleaning and other supplies	3.86%	1.99%	2.04%
Telephone and telegraph	1.89%	2.10%	2.50%
Other operating expenses	3.26%	6.04%	5.39%
Total Operating Expenses	40.43%	54.52%	64.07%
Gross Operating Profit	59.57%	45.48%	35.93%
Capital expenses:			
Real estate and property taxes	4.02%	3.87%	3.68%
Insurance	2.44%	1.86%	1.10%
Interest	12.08%	10.40%	10.86%
Rent	2.88%	5.35%	2.89%
Depreciation & amortization	15.88%	12.22%	12.83%
Total Capital Expenses	37.30%	33.70%	31.36%
NET PROFIT	22.27%	11.78%	4.57%
Average investment per motel:			
Buildings	$ 92,807	$ 714,333	$2,188,481
	21,655	193,158	575,726
Subtotal	$114,462	$ 907,491	$2,764,207
Land	22,908	124,969	456,008
TOTAL INVESTMENT	$137,370	$1,032,460	$3,220,215
General statistics:			
Percentage of occupancy	64.62%	70.32%	54.85%
Avg. daily rate per rented room	$11.73	$14.96	$17.05
Avg. daily rate per guest	$ 6.33	$ 8.33	$10.74
Avg. no. guests per room	1.85	1.80	1.59

 Typical operating percentages
for major hotels and motor hotels

Typical expense ratios on major hotels and motor hotels have apparently been fairly steady in recent years.

Some of the most authoritative and useful reports on hotels and motor hotels come from an international certified public accounting firm with uncommon experience and an uncommon name: Laventhol & Horwath.

Each year, Laventhol & Horwath analyzes operations in selected hotels and motor hotels* in the United States in its report entitled *Lodging Industry*. According to *Lodging Industry* figures on the late 1960s and early 1970s, typical operating ratios—the *percentages* of actual income which are claimed by certain expenses—have not varied a great deal.

Expense ratios set out on the next two pages are averages; variations from one hotel to another can be sizable because of differences in size, age, type, location, and other factors.

Similarly, the average expense ratios of first-class hotels in other countries have apparently been relatively stable in recent years.

Through its more than 50 overseas offices, Laventhol & Horwath also collects data on hotel operations outside the United States. Each year its report, *Worldwide Operating Statistics of the Hotel Industry,* sets out data on selected first-class hotels in many countries.†

On pages 166 and 167 is an interesting summary of operating ratios in the early 1970s. In each annual sampling, there were some important differences from one hotel to another. Yet one sees remarkably little change from year to year in the *average expense percentages.*

One can learn much from this experience report, particularly from various groupings of data by different factors which affect profitability. However, the same caveat applies again here: Such experience data can be extremely helpful, but it alone should not be used in lieu of individual, expert analysis on a specific case.

---

* In its forty-second annual report (1974 edition summarizing 1973 operations), Laventhol & Horwath combined operating figures of hotels and motor hotels for the first time. Reason: It was becoming increasingly difficult to differentiate between the two in a meaningful way.

† For example, the 1974 edition included data on 1973 operations in 272 first-class hotels in over 65 countries. These hotels had more than 80,000 rooms, employed over 90,000 persons, and generated gross revenue exceeding $1 billion (U.S.).

THE LODGING INDUSTRY DOLLAR*

Based upon Operating Results for 1973 and 1972 of
Selected Lodging Industry Establishments

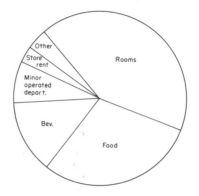

WHERE IT CAME FROM

	1973	1972
Guest room rentals	52.7	52.1
Food sales	27.0	27.1
Beverage sales	12.0	12.2
Telephone sales	2.4	2.4
Store rentals	1.7	1.7
Other sources	4.2	4.5

* Based on the arithmetic mean.
From: Lodging Industry, 1974 edition, with permission of Laventhol & Horwath.

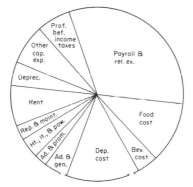

WHERE IT WENT

Payroll and related expenses	36.7	35.9
Food cost	8.4	8.7
Beverage cost	2.6	2.9
Departmental expenses	8.6	8.4
Administrative and general	4.8	4.8
Advertising and promotion	2.5	2.5
Heat, light, and power	3.6	3.5
Repairs and maintenance	2.7	2.7
Rent, municipal taxes, and insurance	14.3	14.8
Interest	4.8	4.6
Depreciation	6.6	6.8
Net income before taxes	4.3	4.4

COMPARATIVE OPERATING FIGURES FOR HOTELS IN EARLY 1970s

All Figures Are Medians

	1972	1971	1970
House income—excluding store rentals			
Ratio to room sales	39 %	33 %	35 %
Ratio to total sales	19	17	19
Rooms			
Percentage of occupancy	62 %	55 %	57 %
Ratios to room sales			
Payroll and related expenses	21.8	22.0	22.4
Other expenses	8.1	8.3	7.9
Departmental income	70.2	69.3	69.1
Restaurant			
Food sales—ratio to room sales	57 %	55 %	56 %
Beverage sales—ratio to food sales	42	43	40
Food cost per dollar sale*	34.1	35.2	34.4
Beverage cost per dollar sale	26.1	27.0	28.3
Ratios to total food and beverage sales			
Payroll and related expenses	43.6	45.7	46.3
Other expenses	9.6	9.7	8.7
Departmental income	16.4	12.4	12.4
Ratio of departmental income to room sales	12.3	9.7	10.6
Sales—ratios to room sales			
Telephone	4.3%	4.5%	4.1%
Valet	.3	.3	.4
Guest laundry	.4	.3	.5

* After credit for employees' meals.
From: Lodging Industry, 1973 edition, with permission of Laventhol & Horwath.

	1972	1971	1970
Telephone departmental loss—ratio to room sales	2.8	2.5	2.1
Income from all sources except rooms, restaurant,			
telephone, and stores—ratio to room sales	2.3	2.5	3.0
Store rentals—ratio to room sales	2.6	3.3	2.4
Ratios to room sales			
Administrative and general expenses	18.6%	18.8%	18.6%
Payroll taxes and employee benefits	11.4	9.9	9.0
Advertising and promotion	7.0	6.4	6.3
Heat, light, and power	8.8	10.6	10.2
Repairs and maintenance	9.5	8.9	9.0
Replacements, improvements, and additions	5.4	4.5	5.8
Ratios to total sales—excluding store rentals			
Payroll (entire hotel)	32.2%	36.2%	36.4%
Employees' meals	1.4	1.3	1.3
Payroll taxes and employee benefits	5.0	5.1	4.7
Total payroll and related expenses	38.8	42.1	43.0
Administrative and general expenses	9.9	10.2	9.7
Advertising and promotion	3.6	3.3	3.2
Heat, light, and power	5.0	4.8	5.2
Repairs and maintenance	4.8	4.8	4.8
Replacements, improvements, and additions	2.6	2.5	2.6

INTERNATIONAL HOTELS

Percentage Distribution of Revenue and
Expenses in the Early 1970s

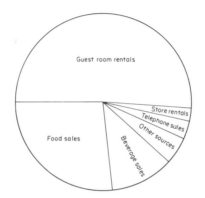

WHERE IT CAME FROM

	1973	1972	1971
Room sales	43.5%	43.0%	44.2%
Food sales	30.5	30.0	29.1
Beverage sales	15.1	14.7	15.2
Minor operated depts.	7.3	8.0	8.3
Store rentals	1.4	1.5	1.4
Other income	2.2	2.8	1.8
	100.0%	100.0%	100.0%

From: Various editions of *Worldwide Operating Statistics of the Hotel Industry,*
with permission of Laventhol & Horwath.

WHERE IT WENT

	1973	1972	1971
Payroll and related expenses	32.0%	30.7%	29.8%
Food cost	10.8	10.4	10.2
Beverage cost	4.0	4.0	4.4
Departmental expenses (includes cost of sales in minor operated depts.)	15.5	14.9	16.5
Administrative and general	4.4	4.2	4.1
Advertising and promotion	2.7	2.5	2.6
Heat, light, and power	3.7	3.5	3.5
Repairs and maintenance	2.8	2.7	2.6
Rent	7.6	7.4	8.2
Depreciation	4.6	4.8	6.0
Other capital expenses	7.2	7.5	7.3
Profit before income tax	4.7	7.4	4.8
	100.0%	100.0%	100.0%

 Typical percentage rents

What rate of percentage rent is reasonable for a particular super-market? Or department store? Or shoe store?

There is a wealth of data available to help you.

Rent can be set as a fixed dollar amount (flat rental), as a percentage of the tenant's sales (percentage rental), or as a combination of the two.

Most owners of tenant-occupied stores look to guaranteed (or flat) rents to pay out of-pocket operating expenses and to meet debt service (principal and interest) payments. However, the difference between a so-so return to the landlord and a very profitable investment is often a good percentage-of-sales clause in the lease. Such clauses usually provide for the tenant to pay the landlord, in addition to the guaranteed rent, a certain percentage of any sales over a specified volume.

Percentage rental agreements are one means of compensating the landlord for the contribution of his location to the tenant's sales. They are also one very important means of adjusting rents to reflect changes in the purchasing power of the dollar; other things being equal, one would expect the dollar amounts of sales to increase in an inflationary period.

In negotiating the percentage clause in a lease, one should have a pretty good idea of what percentages are customary for the same store types in similar locations. There are several excellent guides to the typical rates of percentage rents being used by others:

1. A major source is *Percentage Leases,* published by the Realtors National Marketing Institute (formerly the National Institute of Real Estate Brokers). See Summary A for average percentage rental rates for 97 business types. This excellent study is updated every three years.

2. The most complete and authoritative experience report on U.S. and Canadian shopping centers is the Urban Land Institute's the *Dollars and Cents of Shopping Centers.* Median rates of percentage rents in various types of shopping centers are listed for selected store types in Summaries B1 and B2. ULI publishes an updated edition of this detailed study every three years.

3. Each year the December issue of *Buildings* magazine includes a list of percentage lease rates prevalent in about 20 U.S. cities. See Summary C.

4. Each year Real Estate Research Corporation's *National Market Letter* reports on percentage rental rates for about 50 business types in 1940, 1950, 1960, and the current year.

5. A supplement included each year with the May issue of *Chain Store Age* magazine includes abstracts of recent shopping center leases for several store types. These data can serve as a good supplement to those provided by the ULI and RNMI studies, particularly in the years between new editions.

6. Many real estate professionals have access to data from recent leases or to the leases themselves.

These sources provide some excellent *guides*—but not *rules*—for action. One must remember that there can be reasons for substantial variations in individual cases.

Several property types—banks, car washes, and stamp redemption centers are good examples—are usually omitted from such summaries because percentage rental clauses are not commonly used for them.

SUMMARY A: AVERAGE % RENTAL RATES

Type of store	Average % Rental Rate 1973	1970	Type of Store	Average % Rental Rate 1973	1970
Antique Shops	5.40%		Home Appliances	3.76	
Art Galleries	6.46		Home Improvement Centers	3.61	
Auto Parts	4.64		Hosiery & Lingerie	6.91	7.10
Auto Tire, Battery & Accessory	3.17	2.95%	Ice Cream	5.75	5.82
Bakeries	5.52	5.18	Interior Decoration	6.44	
Barber Shops	7.71	7.68	Jewelry	5.62	5.45
Beauty Shops	7.43	7.78	Junior Department Stores	3.31	
Beauty & Barber Supply	6.04		Key Shops	10.20	
Bed & Bath Shops	6.25		Kiosks	7.62	
Bicycles	5.14		Leather Goods	6.32	7.10
Billiards	9.00	8.00	Lighting Fixtures	6.33	6.00
Books & Stationery	5.80	5.60	Linen	6.00	5.63
Boutiques—*see separate store*			Liquor Stores	4.49	3.82
categories for 1973		6.60	Maternity	5.92	5.93
Bowling Lanes	7.67		Meat Markets	2.38	2.75
Boy's Clothing—*see Children's*			Medical Equipment & Supplies	5.67	5.00
Clothing for 1973		5.40	Men's Apparel—Fashion	5.26	
Boy's Shoes—*see Children's*			Men's Apparel—Casual	5.24	
Shoes for 1973		5.19	Men's Clothing—*see Men's*		
Bridal Shops	5.85	5.25	*Apparel, Fashion & Casual*		
Camera Stores	5.01		*for 1973 figures*		4.85
Candle Shops	6.54		Men's Shoes	5.68	5.66
Candy Stores	7.85	7.98	Movie Theatres	10.24	9.91
Card & Greeting Shops	6.86		Music & Instruments	4.58	4.75
Carpet & Rug	5.25	4.22	Office Supplies	5.22	4.00
Catalog Stores	2.88		Optical	7.38	7.58
Children's Clothing	5.68	6.80	Paint & Wallpaper	5.15	4.00
Children's Shoes	5.64	5.58	Parking Lots & Garages—		
Cigar & Tobacco	6.25	6.55	Non-attended	64.17	62.43
Cocktail Lounges	7.13	7.33	Pet Shops	6.10	5.70
Coin & Stamp Shops	5.75		Photography Studios	6.23	5.87
Cosmetic Stores	6.77		Print Shops	4.67	
Delicatessens	5.30	5.91	Radio & Television	3.51	3.69
Department Stores	2.48	2.83	Record Shops	5.54	5.43
Discount Stores	1.94	1.83	Rental Stores	6.83	5.83
Drapery	5.00	4.78	Restaurants—Family	5.55	5.75
Drive-in Grocery	2.75	2.25	Restaurants—Drive-in	6.41	5.65
Drug Stores	2.88	3.42	Restaurants—With Bar	5.94	6.06
Drug Stores—Pharmacy	3.90	4.44	Sewing Machines	4.09	3.34
Dry Cleaning & Laundry	7.30	7.02	Shoe Repair	8.40	8.31
Dry Cleaning & Laundry—			Sporting Goods Stores	5.06	4.42
Coin-op	7.78	8.52	Sundries	5.00	6.43
Fabric Shops	4.80	4.87	Supermarkets	1.27	1.26
Family Centers	3.00	4.74	Toy Stores	5.50	
Florist & Garden	6.35	6.21	Travel Agencies	7.50	
Furniture	5.22	3.82	Tuxedo & Formal Wear Rental	5.46	
Furriers	6.40	5.83	Uniform	5.50	5.25
Gas Stations	1.65*	1.72*	Variety	3.83	4.01
Gift Shops	6.38	6.35	Western Wear Apparel	5.00	
Gourmet Foods	5.90		Women's Apparel—*see*		
Hair Goods	6.67	6.83	*Women's Apparel, Fashion &*		
Hardware	4.23	3.66	*Casual for 1973 figures*		5.26
Health Foods	5.63	5.85	Women's Apparel—Fashion	5.20	
Health Spas & Clubs	7.23		Women's Apparel—Casual	5.38	
Hobby Crafts	5.71		Women's Shoes	5.45	5.49
Hobby Shops	5.75	5.97			

* Expressed in cents per gallon.

SUMMARY B-1: RATES OF PERCENTAGE RENTS IN U.S. SHOPPING CENTERS

Tenant classification	Regional centers	Community centers	Neighborhood centers
Supermarkets	1.25%	1.13%	1.25%
Restaurants without liquor	6.00	5.00	5.00
Department stores	2.50		
Junior department stores	3.00	3.00	2.50
Variety stores	4.00	4.00	4.00
Ladies' specialty	6.00	5.50	6.00
Ladies' ready-to-wear	5.00	5.00	5.00
Men's wear	5.00	5.00	5.00
Family shoe	6.00	5.00	5.00
Ladies' shoe	6.00	5.00	
Yard goods	5.00	5.00	5.00
Hardware	4.00	4.00	4.00
Drugs	3.00	3.00	3.00
Jewelry	5.00	5.00	5.25
Cards and gifts	7.00	6.00	6.00
Liquor and wine	4.50	4.00	4.50
Beauty shops	8.00	8.00	8.00
Barber shops	8.00	8.00	8.00
Cleaners and dyers	8.00	8.00	8.00
Coin laundries		9.00	10.00

Notes: All percentages above are medians.

The source has data on more than 100 tenant classifications. The author abstracted data on tenants in just 20 classifications which represent the overwhelming majority of shopping center occupancy. Percentage rates in these 20 tenant classifications are based on sampling of over 6,000 stores.

From: Dollars and Cents of Shopping Centers: 1975, reprinted with permission of ULI—the Urban Land Institute, 1200 18th Street, N.W., Washington, D.C. 20036.

SUMMARY B-2: RATES OF PERCENTAGE RENTS IN CANADIAN SHOPPING CENTERS

Tenant classification	Regional centers	Community centers	Neighborhood centers
Supermarkets	1.50%	1.50%	1.00%
Restaurants without liquor	6.00	6.00	6.00
Department stores	1.50		
Junior department stores	5.00	4.25	5.00
Variety stores	6.00	5.00	
Ladies' specialty	6.00	6.00	6.00
Ladies' ready-to-wear	6.00	6.00	6.00
Men's wear	6.00	6.00	6.00
Family shoe	6.00	6.00	6.00
Ladies' shoe	6.00	6.00	6.00
Yard goods	6.00	6.00	6.00
Hardware	5.00	5.00	6.00
Drugs	5.00	4.50	4.50
Jewelry	5.00	6.00	
Cards and gifts	7.00	7.00	6.00
Liquor and wine			
Beauty shops	8.00	8.00	8.50
Barber shops	10.00	10.00	10.00
Cleaners and dyers	8.00	8.00	8.00
Coin laundries			

Notes: All percentages above are medians.
For this summary, the author abstracted median percentages for the same 20 tenant classifications in the preceding summary on U.S. shopping centers. The rates above are based on a sampling of over 1,300 stores.

From: Dollars and Cents of Shopping Centers: 1975, reprinted with permission of ULI—the Urban Land Institute, 1200 18th Street, N.W., Washington, D.C. 20036.

SUMMARY C: PERCENTAGE LEASE TABLES

Type of store	Arthur Rubloff & Co. Chicago, Ill.	Harry Marks Marks Bros. Des Moines, Iowa	Herbert D. Weitzman Henry S. Miller Co. Dallas, Texas	John A. Dodds Reaume & Dodds, Inc. Detroit, Mich.	Ray F. Moseley Moseley & Co. Kansas City, Mo.	Irving L. W. Saperston Saperston Co. Buffalo, N.Y.
Art Shops	8–10	—	6–8	8–10	7–8	8–10
Auto Accessories	4–5	3–4	5	4–6	3–4	3–5
Bakeries	4	5–6	6–8	6–8	4–6	5–6
Barber Shops	8–10	10	7–9	8–10	8–10	8–10
Beauty Shops	8–10	—	6–8	10	8–10	7–10
Books and Stationery	5–6	5¹/₂–7¹/₂	5¹/₂–6	5–8	5–6	5–8
Bowling Lanes	10	—	8–10	—	10	10
Candy	8–10	10	6–7	8–12	6–8	6–10
Children's Clothing	6–8	6–7	5–6¹/₂	4–7	5–7	6–8
Cocktail Lounge	8–10	10	8–10	10	8–10	8–10
Credit Clothing	4–7	6–8	6–6¹/₂	4–5	4–5	5–8
Delicatessen, Specialty Foods	5	—	6–7	8–10	6–7	6–10
Department Stores	2¹/₂–3	2¹/₂–3	2¹/₂–3	2–2¹/₂	2¹/₂–3	2–3
Discount Stores (over 75,000 sq. ft.)	1¹/₂–2	2	2¹/₄–2¹/₂	1¹/₂	1–1¹/₂	1¹/₂–2¹/₂
Discount Stores (under 75,000 sq. ft.)	2	2	2¹/₄–3	5	1¹/₂	2–4
Drug Stores (Chain)	2¹/₂–4	3–4	2¹/₂–4	3–5	2¹/₂–4	3–4
Drug Stores (Individual)	4–6	4–5	3¹/₂–4¹/₂	6	4–5	4–6
Drug Stores (Prescription)	8–10	—	6–8	7–10	—	7–10
Dry Cleaning & Laundry	7–8	—	8–10	8	8–10	6–8
Dry Cleaning & Laundry (Coin Operated)	10	—	9–10	—	8–10	10
Electrical Appliances	3–6	—	5–6	4–6	5–6	4–6
Fabrics	5–6	5–6	4–6	6	—	6–7
Florists	10	8–10	6–7	8–10	7–10	7–10
Florists (Garden Supply)	6	—	6	—	6	6
Furniture	4–6	3–4	3–5	4–6	4–5	3¹/₂–5
Furs	6–8	6–8	6–8	5	6–8	6–8
Garage (Storage)	40–60	40–55	40–55	50	35–50	40–50
Gas Stations, cents per gallon	1¹/₂–2	1¹/₂	1¹/₄–1¹/₂	1–1¹/₂	1¹/₂	1¹/₂
Gift Shops	8–10	8–10	6–8	7–10	6–10	8–10
Grocery Stores (Individual)	1¹/₂–3	—	1¹/₂–2	—	1¹/₂–2	1¹/₂–3
Grocery Stores (Chain)	1–1¹/₂	1¹/₂–2	1¹/₄–1³/₄	1–2	1–1¹/₂	1¹/₂–1³/₄
Hardware	4–5	4–6	4¹/₂–5¹/₂	—	4–5	4–5
Hobby Shops, Toys	6–8	—	5–6	5	8	8–10
Hosiery and Knit Goods	6–8	6–7	6–7	8	5–8	6–8
Jewelry (Costume)	6–10	10	5¹/₂–7¹/₂	8–10	8–10	7–10
Jewelry (Exclusive)	5–8	5–6	6–8	5–8	6–8	6–9

Source: December 1974 issue of *Buildings* magazine, reprinted with permission of the Stamats Publishing Co., 427 Sixth Avenue, S.E., Cedar Rapids, Iowa 52406.

Seattle, Wash.	Kenneth R. Jensen Green Tree Bldg. Management Co. Minneapolis, Minn.	Bernard Grossman Feist & Feist New York, N.Y.	Marvin S. Schwartz Lewis & Fink Cleveland, Ohio	Albert R. Bullier, Sr. Bullier & Bullier Portland, Ore.	Maury L. Rosenberg Binswanger Herman Company Philadelphia, Pa.	George T. Fritts J. B. & W. G. Brownlow Knoxville, Tenn.	Joseph E. Chotiner Oxford Development Co. Pittsburgh, Pa.
—	10	8–10	6–8	7–10	8–10	—	8–10
—	5	3–4	3–5	4–5	4–5	—	3–4
4–6	5	5–6	5–6	4–5	4–6	—	6–8
8–10	10	8–10	8–10	9–10	8–10	—	8–10
8–10	10	8–10	8–10	9–10	8–10	—	8–10
6–10	6	5–6	5–8	5–7	6–8	—	5–6
—	10	8–10	9–10	9–10	10		—
—	8	8	6–10	6–8	8–12	10	8–10
—	6	4–6	5–6	5–7	4–7	8	5–6
6	10	8–10	7–8	8–9	8	—	5–6
—	6	6–7	4–5	4–6	4–8	—	—
—	6	4–7	4–6	5	4–5	—	6
—	2^1/$_2$–3	2–3	2–2^1/$_2$	2^1/$_2$–3	2–3^1/$_2$	3–4	1^1/$_2$–2^1/$_2$
—	1^1/$_2$	1^1/$_2$–2	1–1^1/$_2$	1^1/$_2$–2	1^1/$_2$–2	—	—
	1^1/$_2$–2	1^1/$_2$–2	1^1/$_2$–2	2	1^1/$_2$	—	—
—	2^1/$_2$–3^1/$_2$	3	2^1/$_2$–4	2^1/$_2$–3^1/$_2$	3–4	4–5	4
7	5	4–5	3–5	3^1/$_2$–5^1/$_2$	4–6	5	—
—	8–10	6–8	5–8	8–10	5	—	—
—	8	6–8	6–8	8–10	8–10	—	8–10
—	10	8–9	8–10	10	10	—	—
—	4–5	3–4	3–5	3–5	4–6	—	4–5
—	6	5–6	5–7	4–6	6–8	—	6
6	10	8–9	8–10	7–10	8–10	—	8–10
—	6	5–6	5–6	5–6	—	—	6
6–10	5	3–4	4–5	4–5	4–5	4–5	3^1/$_2$–5
6	6–8	6–8	6–8	6	6–8	—	6
40–55	50	40–50	40–50	40–85	50	—	—
1^1/$_2$	2^1/$_2$	1^1/$_2$	1–2	1–2	1–1^1/$_2$	—	—
8–10	8–10	8–10	7–8	7–10	8–10	—	8–10
—	3	2–3	1^1/$_4$–2^1/$_2$	1^1/$_2$–3	2–3	—	—
—	1–1^1/$_2$	1^1/$_4$–1^1/$_2$	1–1^1/$_2$	1–1^1/$_2$	1^1/$_4$–2	—	1^1/$_2$–2
—	5–7	4–5	3^1/$_2$–5	3^1/$_2$–5	4–6	—	4–6
—	6–8	6–8	6–8	6–8	6–7	—	6–8
—	8	6–8	7–8	5–7	6–8	10	6
—	10	8–10	7–8	8	8–10	—	8–10
7–8	8–10	5–6	7–10	5–7	4–6	—	4–6

(Cont.)

SUMMARY C: PERCENTAGE LEASE TABLES
(Cont.)

Type of store	Arthur Rubloff & Co. Chicago, Ill.	Harry Marks Marks Bros. Des Moines, Iowa	Herbert D. Weitzman Henry S. Miller Co. Dallas, Texas	John A. Dodds Reaume & Dodds, Inc. Detroit, Mich.	Ray F. Moseley Moseley & Co. Kansas City, Mo.	Irving L. W. Saperston Saperston Co. Buffalo, N.Y.
Leather Goods	6–8	—	5–7	6	6–8	7–8
Liquors and Wines	2–4	5	3^1/$_2$–5	—	4–5	4–5
Meat Markets (Individual)	4–5	—	3^1/$_2$	3–4	—	3–4
Meat Markets (Chain)	4	—	2^1/$_2$	3–4	3–4	4–5
Men's Clothing	4–7	5–6	5–6	5–6	4–5	5–7
Men's Furnishings	6–8	6	5–6	6–8	5–7	7–8
Men's Hats	8	7–8	5–7	5–7	7–8	6–7
Men's Shoes	6–7	6–7	6–6^1/$_2$	5–7	5–6	6–8
Men's Shoes (Volume)	6	6–7	4–6	5–6	4–5	4–7
Millinery	10–15	10–12	6–7	8–11	10–12	10–12
Motion Picture Theaters	12^1/$_2$–15	—	10–12	5–7	10	10–15
Office Supply	5–6	5–6	5–6	5–7	5–6	5–6
Optical	8–10	8–10	7–10	8–10	8–10	8–10
Paint, Wallpaper Supplies	4–6	—	5–5^1/$_2$	6	4–5	4–6
Parking Lots & Garages (Attendant)	40–65	40–60	40–55	50–60	40–50	40–60
Parking Lots & Garages (Non-Attendant)	60–70	45–60	60–65	—	60–65	60–70
Photography	6–10	6	5–6	8	6–10	6–10
Pianos and Musical Instruments	4–6	—	5–5^1/$_2$	6	6–8	4–7
Radio, Television, Hi-Fi	3–5	3–5	5–6	6	4–5	4–5
Record Shops	5–6	5–6	5^1/$_2$–6^1/$_2$	6–7	6–7	5–7^1/$_2$
Restaurants	5–7	5–6	6–10	6–8	5–6	6–10
Restaurants (with Bar)	7–8	—	6–8	5–8	6–8	6–10
Shoe Repair	10	—	7–9	8–10	8–10	10
Sporting Goods	6–8	6–8	5–6	6–8	6–8	6–8
Wig Shops	10	—	6–8	5–8	10	—
Women's Dress Shops	4–8	5–6	4^1/$_2$–6^1/$_2$	4–8	4–6	4–6
Women's Furnishings	6–7	6	4^1/$_2$–6^1/$_2$	5–10	6–8	6–7
Women's Shoes	6–7	5–6	6–6^1/$_2$	6	5–7	5–7
5–10¢ or 25¢–$2 Stores	4–5	3–4	4–5	5	3–4	3–5

Seattle, Wash.	Kenneth R. Jensen Green Tree Bldg. Management Co. Minneapolis, Minn.	Bernard Grossman Feist & Feist New York, N.Y.	Marvin S. Schwartz Lewis & Fink Cleveland, Ohio	Albert R. Bullier, Sr. Bullier & Bullier Portland, Ore.	Maury L. Rosenberg Binswanger Herman Company Philadelphia, Pa.	George T. Fritts J. B. & W. G. Brownlow Knoxville, Tenn.	Joseph E. Chotiner Oxford Development Co. Pittsburgh, Pa.
—	6–8	6–7	6–8	6–8	6–8	7	6
—	5	3–5	—	—	4–6	6	—
—	6	4–5	3–4	4–5	4–5	—	3–4
—	3	3–4	2–3	3–5	4–6	—	—
3–4$1/2$	4–6	5–6	5–6	4–6	6–8	7	6
3–4$1/2$	6–8	6–7	6–8	6–8	6–8	7	6–8
3–4$1/2$	8	6–7	7–8	8	6–8	—	—
3–4$1/2$	6–8	6–7	5–6	6	5–6	7	6
—	6	6	4–5	6	5–6	7	6
—	10	8	10	10–15	8–10	7–10	6–8
15	10–12	10–12$1/2$	7–15	10–12$1/2$	10–12$1/2$	—	10–15
—	5	5–7	6–7	5	5–6	—	6
6	8–10	6–10	8–10	6–10	8–10	—	6–10
—	6	4–6	5–7	5–6	5–7	—	5–6
40–55	10–60	50–60	40–50	40–60	50–80	40–60	—
—	60–70	60–70	60–65	75–85	60–80	—	—
6	10	0–10	8–10	0–8	7–8	—	8–10
—	5	3–6	6–7	4–6	5–7	—	4–6
—	5	4–5	3–5	3–5	4–5	—	4–6
6	6	5–6	5–6	5–6	5–6	6	6–7
5–6	6–7	6–10	5–6	5–6	4–6	5–7	5–7
5–6	8–9	6–7	6–7	5–8	8–10	—	6
—	6–8	8–10	10	10	8–10	—	6
—	5–6	3–4	5–6	4–6	5–6	—	6
—	10	7	8–10	10–15	—	—	—
4$1/2$–6	3–5	4–6	5–6	4–7	5–6	6–8	5–6
—	6	5–8	6–7	5–7	5–8	—	5–6
—	5–6	6–7	5–6	5–7	5–7	6	6
—	5	4–5	3–4	3–5	3–5	5	—

(Cont.)

SUMMARY C: PERCENTAGE LEASE TABLES

(Cont.)

Type of store	J. B. Grimmer Grimmer Realty Co. Birmingham, Ala.	Roy P. Drachman Roy Drachman Realty Tucson, Ariz.	Coldwell, Banker & Co. Los Angeles, Calif.	James J. Cordano James J. Cordano Co. Sacramento, Calif.	Henry H. Wright Stockton, Whatley, Davin & Co. Jacksonville, Fla.	Melton D. Haney Charles E. Smith Mgt. Inc. Washington, D.C.
Art Shops	6	6	6–8	6–8	6	8–10
Auto Accessories	3–4	3–5	3–5	3–4	$2^1/2$	—
Bakeries	6	5–6	4–7	5–6	6	6–8
Barber Shops	8–10	7–10	8–10	8–10	—	8–9
Beauty Shops	8–10	8–10	8–10	8–10	6	6–9
Books and Stationery	4–6	5–6	5–7	5–6	6	6–8
Bowling Lanes	8–10	7–8	6–8	8–10	—	—
Candy	6–8	7–9	6–9	6–10	7	7–9
Children's Clothing	5–6	5–7	5–7	5–7	6	5–6
Cocktail Lounge	6–10	5–6	6–7	6–8	—	8–10
Credit Clothing	5	5–6	5–7	5–6	—	6–7
Delicatessen, Specialty Foods	6	5–6	6–8	6–7	5–6	$5^1/2$–6
Department Stores	$1^1/2$–3	2–3	—	6–7	$1^1/2$–3	$1^1/2$–$2^1/2$
Discount Stores (over 75,000 sq. ft.)	2	1–$1^1/2$	1–$1^1/2$	$1^1/2$	—	$1^1/2$–2
Discount Stores (under 75,000 sq. ft.)	2	1–2	2	$1^1/2$–2	—	$1^1/2$–2
Drug Stores (Chain)	$2^1/2$–3	$1^1/2$–$3^1/2$	2–4	2–4	3–4	4–6
Drug Stores (Individual)	3–5	4–5	4–6	4–6	4	—
Drug Stores (Prescription)	5	6–7	6	6–8	—	—
Dry Cleaning & Laundry	7–8	5–8	7–10	7–10	5	4–6
Dry Cleaning & Laundry (Coin Operated)	10	6–8	6–8	6–8	—	7–8
Electrical Appliances	3–5	4–5	3–5	3–5	4–5	—
Fabrics	5–6	5–6	6	5–6	5–6	4–6
Florists	6	7–9	8–10	8–10	6	6–8
Florists (Garden Supply)	4	5–6	5–7	5–6	—	—
Furniture	4–5	4–5	4–6	3–6	—	4–6
Furs	—	5–6	6–8	6–8	—	6–8
Garage (Storage)	—	30–40	40–50	30–50	—	—
Gas Stations, cents per gallon	1–2	$1^1/2$–2	1–2	1–2	$1^1/2$	1–2
Gift Shops	6–8	6–8	6–9	6–9	6	7–9
Grocery Stores (Individual)	$1^1/2$–2	$1^1/2$–2	4–6	2–4	—	—
Grocery Stores (Chain)	1–$1^1/2$	1–$1^1/2$	$1^1/2$–2	$1^1/2$–2	1	1–$1^1/2$

Type of store	J. B. Grimmer Grimmer Realty Co. Birmingham, Ala.	Roy P. Drachman Roy Drachman Realty Tucson, Ariz.	Coldwell, Banker & Co. Los Angeles, Calif.	James J. Cordano James J. Cordano Co. Sacramento, Calif.	Henry H. Wright Stockton, Whatley, Davin & Co. Jacksonville, Fla.	Melton D. Haney Charles E. Smith Mgt. Inc. Washington, D.C.
Hardware	4–5	4–5	4–6	4–6	4–5	4–6
Hobby Shops, Toys	5–6	5–7	6–8	6–7	5–6	7–8
Hosiery and Knit Goods	6	6	8	7–10	7	7–8
Jewelry (Costume)	6–7	7–10	7–10	8–10	—	8–10
Jewelry (Exclusive)	4–5	6	6–9	6–8	4$^1/2$	8–9
Leather Goods	5–6	5–6	7–9	6–8	—	7–8
Liquors and Wines	4	4–6	4–6	4–6	2	3–5
Meat Markets (Individual)	—	4–5	3–5	3–5	—	—
Meat Markets (Chain)	—	—	3–4	3–4	—	—
Men's Clothing	4–6	5–6	5–6	5–6	3$^1/2$–6	5–6
Men's Furnishings	6	4–6	6–8	6–8	3$^1/2$–6	5–6
Men's Hats	—	—	10	10	—	5–6
Men's Shoes	6	6–7	6–8	6	5–6	5–7
Men's Shoes (Volume)	6	5–6	5	5–6	6	—
Millinery	6–10	6–8	10	8–10	5–8	—
Motion Picture Theatres	8 10	10–12	7–11	10	—	12$^1/2$
Office Supply	—	5 6	5–7	5–6	—	5–7
Optical	6–10	7–8	9–11	8–10	10	8–10
Paint, Wallpaper Supplies	4–5	4–7	3–6	3–7	3	6–7
Parking Lots & Garages (Attendant)	50	40–50	45–55	40–50	—	40–50
Parking Lots & Garages (Non-Attendant)	—	50–60	60–65	50–60	—	40–60
Photography	6	6–10	7–10	7–10	6	7–8
Pianos and Musical Instruments	6	4–6	5	3–6	4	6–8
Radio, Television, Hi-Fi	5–6	5–6	4–6	4–6	4–5	6–7
Record Shops	6	6–7	6–8	6–8	6	6–7
Restaurants	4–6	5–7	5 6	5–6	5–6	5–7
Restaurants (With Bar)	6–8	5–7	5–7	5–7	—	6–8
Shoe Repair	8–10	6–8	8–10	8–10	—	8–10
Sporting Goods	5–6	4–6	5–7	5–7	6	6–8
Wig Shops	6–10	8–10	—	7–10	5–6	6–8
Women's Dress Shops	4–6	4–6	5–7	5–7	4–7	6–8
Women's Furnishings	4–6	5–7	5–7	5–7	3$^1/2$–6	6–8
Women's Shoes	6	5–6	6–7	6	5–6	6–8
5–10¢ or 25¢–$2 Stores	4–5	3–5	3–5	3–5	3–4	4–6

56

$1/gallon/month
for service stations

Some buyers of operating service stations use this guide to value: One dollar for each gallon of gasoline sold in the average month.

As a guide to real estate value, this rule of thumb has some serious weaknesses.

Say Mr. A. pumped 1,200,000 gallons in his station last year. Now A wants to sell the station and retire. Mr. B., who owns a small chain of independent (cut-rate) stations, is interested in buying A's station. Being well-informed in his field, B is familiar with this rule of thumb which suggests a price of (100,000 gallons in the average month @ $1) $100,000. However, since he *is* well-informed, B knows that gallonage alone is not a reliable guide to real estate value; B also wants answers to these questions:

1. To what extent have A's prices affected gallonage? (After all, B's goal is *profit,* not just volume.)

2. Has gallonage been affected by other inducements such as trading stamps or "free" merchandise?

3. To what extent was patronage the result of A's management ability (goodwill)—an important factor in service station operation?

4. Was much of this gallonage pumped during unusual hours? (Certainly, staying open around the clock and on holidays will boost gallonage—as well as costs and problems—but does this increase necessarily mean that the real estate is worth proportionately more?)

5. What potential is there for income from sources other than fuel sales? (Are there service bays? What about sales of other products?)

6. What about the age and condition of these improvements? (Are repairs and replacements needed now? Will they be needed soon?)

7. Are expenses for this particular property uncommonly high or low? (An unusual real estate tax burden is an obvious example.)

8. Is competition likely to increase? (Is this the best site? Are other sites readily available nearby? Is there a ban on more stations?)

9. Is the potential here growing or dwindling? (It's not really last year B is interested in; it's the years ahead.)

10. Are land values in the neighborhood increasing or decreasing?

11. Is there surplus land here that could be sold off or used for production of additional income?

12. Could B invest this money in another operating station or build a new one to better advantage?

Depending upon the answers to these and some other questions, B might not want this station for $50,000 or he might well feel justified in paying $150,000 or more.

While this rule of thumb is used by some experienced service station people, it is no better than a *very* rough preliminary guide.

 Types of stores suitable for
particular types of locations

In shopping areas, some types of stores are usually considered suitable for choice (or 100 percent) locations. Others are not.

On the next three pages, over 100 store types are classified by the type of location considered most suitable for each.

Grouping stores so that they are in appropriate locations and are likely to work well together is a challenging problem even for experts.

Some very useful guidelines are set out in this authoritative list by the Community Builders Council of the Urban Land Institute.

LIST OF STORES BY LOCATIONS

For reference purposes, the alphabetically arranged lists below represent a checklist of stores that the Council considers are suitable for the several categories of real estate location in **shopping areas.**

NO. 1 LOCATIONS

(100 Percent or "Hot Spot")

1. Bakery
2. Boys' Clothing
3. Candy Store
4. Children's Wear
5. Cosmetics and Perfume
6. Costume Jewelry
7. Department Store
8. Drugstore
9. Five and Ten
10. Florist
11. Gift Shop
12. Girls' Apparel
13. Grocery (Cash and Carry)
14. Handkerchiefs and Handbags
15. Hosiery Shop
16. Infants' Wear
17. Jewelry
18. Lingerie
19. Leather Goods and Luggage—
   (Depends on ability to pay high rent)
20. Men's Furnishings
21. Men's Clothing
22. Millinery
23. Novelties
24. Optical Shop
25. Paperback Bookstore
26. Photographic Supplies and Cameras
27. Popcorn and Nuts
28. Prescriptions (May not be possible because of drug store)
29. Restaurant
30. Shoes, Women's
31. Shoes, Men's
32. Shoes, Children's
33. Sportswear, Women's
34. Tobacconist
35. Toilet Goods
36. Variety Store
37. Women's Wear

The following shops may go equally well in either No. 1 or No. 2 locations:

1. Cafeteria
2. Dry Goods
3. Newsstand
4. Service Grocery

No. 1 locations should be held largely for shops that keep open on certain common nights.

NO. 2 LOCATIONS

(Near the 100 percent area)

1. Art Store and Artists' Supplies
2. Athletic Goods
3. Auto Supplies
4. Bank

(Cont.)

LISTS OF STORES BY LOCATIONS
(Cont.)

A bank should not be in a No. 1 location, as it has limited open hours and when closed has a deadening effect on adjacent shops.

5. Bar (Liquor)

6. Barber Shop (Basement in the No. 1 Location)

When deciding on width of a barber shop, consider carefully the number of lines of barber chairs in order that space will not be wasted.

7. Beauty Shop
8. Bookstore
9. China and Silver
10. Cleaners and Dyers (Pick-Up)
11. Cocktail Lounge
12. Corset Shop
13. Delicatessen (Also in No. 1 location in some cases)
14. Electrical Appliances
15. Fruit and Vegetable Market (Should be considered in relation to regular grocer)
16. Glass and China

17. Laundry Agency
18. Linen Shop
19. Liquor Store
20. Maternity Clothes
21. Pen Shop
22. Radio and Television
23. Sewing Machines and Supplies
24. Sporting Goods
25. Stationery and Greeting Cards
26. Telegraph Office
27. Theater (or No. 3 location)
28. Woolens and Yarns

The following shops may go equally well in either No. 2 or No. 3 locations.

1. Gas, Power and Light Company Offices

2. Ticket Offices
3. Toy Shop

NO. 3 LOCATIONS

1. Army Goods Store (or in No. 4 location)
2. Art Needlework Shop
3. Baby Furniture
4. Building and Loan Office

5. Chinese Restaurant
6. Christian Science Reading Room (or 2nd floor in No. 2)
7. Dance Studio (or No. 4 location)
8. Doctors and Dentists

Doctors and dentists are not favored in central locations. Janitorial expense for doctors' offices is at least twice as high as for ordinary office space. Also, they are hard tenants to please as to maintenance.

9. Drapery and Curtain Shop
10. Electric Equipment and Repair
11. Express Office (A popular service that helps build up a retail area)
12. Furniture (Pays low rent per square foot)
13. Hardware
14. Health Foods Store
15. Hobby Shop
16. Interior Decoration
17. Ladies' and Men's Tailor (or 2nd floor in No. 1 or No. 2 locations)
18. Mortgage Loan Office (or 2nd floor in No. 2 location)
19. Office Supplies and Office Furniture (Pays low rent per square foot)
20. Optometrist and Optician (or No. 1 or 2)
21. Paint Store
22. Photographers (or 2nd floor in No. 1 or No. 2 locations)
23. Piano Store (Low rent)
24. Pictures and Framing (Low rent)
25. Post Office
26. Power and Light Offices
27. Real Estate Offices (or No. 4)
28. Shoe Repair
29. Tavern
30. Ticket Offices
31. Travel Bureau (or No. 2 location)

NO. 4 LOCATIONS

1. Automatic Family Laundry Service
2. Bowling Alleys
3. Carpets and Rugs, Oriental
4. Diaper Service
5. Dog or Cat Hospital (without outside runs)
6. Drive-In Eating Places
7. Radio and Television Broadcasting Station

From: The Community Builders Handbook, reprinted with permission of ULI—the Urban Land Institute, 1200 18th Street, N.W., Washington, D.C. 20036.

Part V

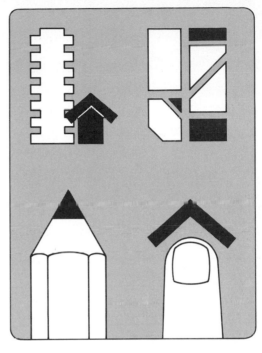

Potpourri

*Private property began the instant somebody had a
mind of his own.*
—E. E. CUMMINGS

58 How to tell real estate from personal property

Is it real estate or it is personal property?

There are three tests.

A growing tree (normally real estate) is cut down, and the log (usually personal property) is cut into 2 × 4's (usually personal property), which are then used to frame a new house (once again, normally real estate).

These examples are fairly obvious. Unfortunately, classifying items as realty or personalty is not always so easy. What about a mirror hung on a wall? What about carpet installed by a tenant? What about a crane in a factory?

How does one decide?

Well, it helps to know the basic distinctions between real estate and personal property. In simplest terms, realty is the land and everything annexed permanently to it. The chief characteristics of real estate are its fixity of location (immobility) and its tangibility. Everything else—everything which can be treated as a thing and owned and is not realty—is personalty. The chief characteristic of personal property is its mobility, and personal property may be intangible.

It also helps to know the three main tests, which have been recognized for decades:

1. *In what manner was the item in question annexed?* If the item cannot be removed from the premises without substantial damage to the real estate, there is a strong suggestion that the item is part of the real estate. A mirror fastened to the wall with twelve barbed nails would more likely be considered a permanent fixture (former item of personal property, now a part of the real estate) than a mirror hung with a single screw.

   A popular misconception—even among real estate professionals—is that an item must be *attached* to the real estate if it is to be considered a part of it. However, courts have held otherwise; it may be enough that there is *constructive* attachment or special adaptation. Thus, the key to a building may be deemed a fixture; and, in a surprising decision in a condemnation case, the doorman's uniform was adjudged a fixture.

2. *What was the intention of the person who originally installed the item?* This may be the most persuasive test of all: Was there intent to annex the item *permanently*? If a tenant installs carpeting and has the right to remove it spelled out in the lease, the tenant's intent that the carpeting *not* be *permanently* installed would seem to be at least implied.

3. *How much continuity of purpose is there between the item in question and the rest of the property?* A traveling crane built to unusual specifications to function in a particular building may be adjudged a (permanent) fixture even though it could be moved away readily.

It also helps to recognize that the classification of an item as realty or personalty is a question of *law* and not a question of *fact.* While the courts may be consistent in *recognizing* these three tests, they are not so consistent in *applying* them. Therefore, any examples like those in the summary on the next page must be recognized as illustrative, not definitive; any particular question of classification that is important should be referred to a lawyer.

It also helps to know the customs, if they are established for particular items. One might be able to remove shutters as simply as, say, pictures; but that would be contrary to established local custom in most areas.

A lot of trouble can be avoided by treating certain items specifically in writing. The appraiser should state which items are included in his valuation. In real estate agreements—listing agreements, sales agreements, leases, and mortgages to name the most obvious—statements to the effect that certain questionable or unusual items were included or excluded can be very useful.

REAL ESTATE OR PERSONAL PROPERTY?

Most often, these items are considered part of the real estate . . .	while these are not.
Mines	Ore (extracted)
Landscaping (planted, growing)	Potted plants
Central air conditioning systems (installed)	Window units (portable)
Furnaces (installed)	Portable heaters
Murals	Pictures
Shutters (installed)	Drapes
Countertop ranges (installed)	Stoves (freestanding)
Tub enclosures (installed)	Shower curtains
Lighting fixtures (installed)	Floor lamps
Incinerators (installed)	Incinerators (portable outdoor)
Dishwasher (built-in)	Dishwasher (portable)
Partitions (conventional, built-in)	Bankers-type (portable) partitions
Kitchen cabinets (built-in)	Buffets (unattached)
Floor tiles (installed)	Rugs (loose)
Hot-water heater (installed)	Plug-in appliances
Theater stages (built-in)	Projection equipment
Concrete sign bases (built-in)	Signs
Craneways (built-in)	Cranes (mobile)
Concrete pump islands	Service station pumps
Leasehold estates	Stocks and bonds

59   Assessed value vs. market value

One should not rely on the real estate tax assessor's valuation of a property as a guide to that property's market value.

Assessor's valuations for real estate tax purposes are often shockingly out of line with market values.

This has been demonstrated in study after study. In one, property assessments in a southern district were reported to range from 1 to 550 percent of market value.

Why are property tax "values" often so far out of line with market values? Here are some of the reasons:

1. In most states, assessors are elected and are not required to have any professional qualifications or experience whatever. Some assessors are highly qualified professionals. Many are not.

2. A large percentage of assessors don't have enough support to do their jobs well. Some can't afford a qualified staff or proper equipment. Many assessors are part-timers. When assessment work is "farmed out" to mass appraisal firms, the average fee is something on the order of $10 per parcel—too meager in most cases to permit the work to be done well by qualified professionals.

3. Partly as a result of the foregoing, buildings are "appraised" without interior inspections and with only the most cursory exterior inspections. Farms are sometimes "valued" without someone even walking the farm. Income properties are regularly valued by people with only a fairly primitive grasp of the income approach. Precomputed tables and rules of thumb are regularly substituted for professional judgment.

4. It is a common practice for assessors to undervalue most of the parcels in their districts in order to make taxpayers think they are getting a break.

5. In many cases, assessors are bound by state laws and administrative regulations* to place "values" on some types of parcels which are much less than their market value.

In addition to all of this, remember that there can be an inverse relationship between assessed value and market value; *other things being equal,* the higher the real estate tax assessment, the lower the market value.

---

* For example, differential assessment procedures on farms and open space.

 Farm values per acre

Want to know how much a farm is worth?

Per-acre figures are available to you from the U.S. government, but they have some serious limitations.

First some good news: You can obtain figures on the average value of farm real estate (land and buildings) per acre for any county or any state.

And then some bad news: These figures are not reliable guides to the value of an individual farm.

Every five years, the Bureau of the Census sets out what are supposed to be average per-acre farm values for each county and for each state. On the next page, by way of illustration, are 1969 figures for farms in Ohio. If you put much stock in these figures—as, alas, some appraisers and assessors seem to do—you can be awfully wrong. Consider:

1. These figures are averages of the *opinions* of farm owners and tenants—not of objective market data. ("Please enter your estimate of the current market value of the acres you operated . . . and the buildings on them.")

2. These figures are out of date by the time they are issued. For example, 1969 figures were issued in 1972, and farm prices had changed in the interim by as much as 30 percent in some areas.

3. Even within the same county, per-acre farm values can vary widely. (What is the size of the farm? Is it irrigated? Is it entirely cleared? Is it near a growing urban center? Is it subject to flooding? What crops can it support? What is the nature of the improvements?)

While these figures can be interesting for general perspective, one should not take them for more than they are: out-of-date averages of opinions.

Somewhat more timely and more reliable are U.S. Department of Agriculture figures which are published twice each year and which are partly based on objective data. USDA sets out an average per-acre price index for each state as of May and November. These USDA reports are the sources of articles like the one below which one sees so often in newspapers and real estate periodicals:

FARMLAND VALUES MAKE RECORD SPURT
The farmland you bought for $1,000 an acre in March 1973 would have cost 25 percent more—or $1,250—had you waited another year.

That, at least, was the average percentage hike in farm real estate values across the Nation, according to a USDA survey for the year ended March 1, 1974.

The leap in farmland values vaulted the per-acre figure to $310 in March 1974 and was the biggest increase ever for a 12-month reporting period . . .

Unfortunately, the USDA indexes are prepared only on a state-by-state basis. Even from one county to another, variations in farm values can be huge. If one assumes that the unit value of a particular farm is necessarily near the statewide average, one can be wrong by several hundred percent.

In summaries at the end of this chapter are USDA indexes for each state from 1912 through 1974. USDA itself has suggested the following as ways in which you can use these indexes:

1. Deriving a current value for a property having a known value in an earlier period.

$$\frac{\text{Index of current year}}{\text{Index of earlier period}} \times \frac{\text{known value in}}{\text{earlier period}} = \frac{\text{estimated}}{\text{current value}}$$

2. Deriving the value of a property in an earlier period when the current value is known.

$$\frac{\text{Index of earlier period}}{\text{Index of current year}} \times \frac{\text{known current}}{\text{value}} = \frac{\text{estimated}}{\text{earlier value}}$$

3. Providing a basis for determining a price at a subsequent settlement date for property acquired in current period.

$$\frac{\text{Index in subsequent year}}{\text{Index at time of contract}} \times \frac{\text{current value}}{\text{at time of contract}} = \frac{\text{settlement}}{\text{price}}$$

4. Adjusting the cash rental rate of a long-term lease to keep the ratio of gross rent to market value constant.

$$\frac{\text{Index in subsequent year}}{\text{Index at time of contract}} \times \frac{\text{cash rent}}{\text{at time of contract}} = \frac{\text{adjusted}}{\text{cash rent}}$$

5. Adjusting the assessed value of farm real estate to reflect change in market values since an earlier assessment.

$$\frac{\text{Index in current year}}{\text{Index in earlier assessment period}} \times \frac{\text{assessed value}}{\text{in earlier period}} = \frac{\text{estimated current}}{\text{assessed value}}$$

Well, these applications have the virtue of simplicity—even if they lack validity. If one of these adjustments suggested by USDA is to be accurate and valid, one must assume that the value of the subject property is necessarily *changing at the same rate as the average for all farms in the state.* This, of course, is a risky assumption—one which would seem to be contradicted by experience and even by some USDA publications.

What these USDA figures *do* give us is a picture—a picture painted in rather broad brush strokes—of what is happening to farm values over time.

USDA's index of average per-acre farm value in the 48 conterminous states rose by 72 percent between March 1960 and March 1970 and by another 60 percent between March 1970 and March 1974. This vigorous appreciation in value is one reason so many investors in farm land are willing to accept rates of return (in terms of farm income) which seem so relatively low.

AVERAGE FARM VALUES IN OHIO
1969 U.S. CENSUS OF AGRICULTURE

County	Average value per acre (land and bldgs.)	County	Average value per acre (land and bldgs.)
Adams	$ 193	Logan	$ 338
Allen	496	Lorain	608
Ashland	319	Lucas	880
Ashtabula	286	Madison	487
Athens	149	Mahoning	422
Auglaize	460	Marion	391
Belmont	155	Medina	518
Brown	302	Meigs	155
Butler	639	Mercer	470
Carroll	185	Miami	583
Champaign	416	Monroe	122
Clark	533	Montgomery	873
Clermont	442	Morgan	120
Clinton	451	Morrow	306
Columbiana	275	Muskingum	180
Coshocton	218	Noble	120
Crawford	381	Ottawa	604
Cuyahoga	2,450	Paulding	360
Darke	476	Perry	187
Defiance	375	Pickaway	410
Delaware	441	Pike	167
Erie	593	Portage	474
Fairfield	390	Preble	457
Fayette	458	Putnam	530
Franklin	951	Richland	337
Fulton	548	Ross	274
Gallia	171	Sandusky	543
Geauga	465	Scioto	220
Greene	611	Seneca	406
Guernsey	143	Shelby	413
Hamilton	803	Stark	539
Hancock	449	Summit	1,101
Hardin	387	Trumbull	363
Harrison	124	Tuscarawas	255
Henry	543	Union	405
Highland	276	Van Wert	486
Hocking	162	Vinton	109
Holmes	254	Warren	611
Huron	319	Washington	179
Jackson	154	Wayne	442
Jefferson	160	Williams	366
Knox	255	Wood	592
Lake	1,157	Wyandot	411
Lawrence	208		
Licking	333		

FARM REAL ESTATE

Index Numbers of Average Value per Acre, by States, Grouped by
Farm Production Regions, 1912–72   1967 = 100

Date[1]	U.S.[2]		Maine	N.H.	Vt.	Mass.	R.I.	Conn.	N.Y.	N.J.	Pa.	Del.	Md.
						Northeast							
1912	22		38	33	30	32	23	22	34	15	25	19	14
1913	23		39	35	30	32	24	23	34	15	25	19	15
1914	24		37	35	29	33	23	23	35	16	25	19	15
1915	24		37	35	31	32	24	23	34	15	25	19	15
1916	25		37	34	34	32	25	23	35	16	26	20	16
1917	27		42	36	37	35	26	25	37	17	29	22	17
1918	30		44	38	39	37	28	26	39	18	30	23	19
1919	33		48	40	40	38	29	28	40	18	31	24	20
1920	40		54	44	44	45	31	31	45	20	35	26	24
1921	37		50	43	44	43	31	31	42	20	33	24	21
1922	32		48	43	43	43	30	32	40	19	30	22	21
1923	31		49	38	39	43	29	31	39	18	30	22	20
1924	30		48	38	38	42	30	32	38	18	29	20	19
1925	29		47	38	37	43	30	31	38	19	29	21	19
1926	29		48	39	37	43	31	31	37	20	29	21	19
1927	28		47	39	37	42	31	31	37	20	28	21	18
1928	27		47	39	36	42	32	32	36	19	28	21	18
1929	27		47	38	36	42	32	32	36	19	27	21	18
1930	26		47	38	36	42	32	32	35	19	27	21	18
1931	24		47	38	36	42	31	32	33	19	25	20	18
1932	20		42	35	33	39	30	30	31	18	24	18	15
1933	16		36	32	30	36	28	28	28	17	20	15	13
1934	17		36	31	29	36	28	28	28	17	20	15	13
1935	18		36	31	30	36	28	28	29	17	21	15	13
1936	18		36	32	30	36	28	28	29	17	22	16	14
1937	19		37	32	30	36	28	29	29	18	22	16	14
1938	19		37	32	29	37	28	28	30	18	22	17	15
1939	19		36	32	29	36	28	28	29	18	22	17	15
1940	19		36	33	30	37	28	28	29	18	23	17	15
1941	19		36	33	30	36	29	29	29	19	23	18	15
1942 Mar.	21		37	33	30	37	30	30	30	20	24	18	16
Nov.	21		38	33	30	37	30	30	30	20	24	19	16
1943 Mar.	23		38	34	32	37	30	30	33	21	26	20	18
Nov.	24		40	36	33	38	32	32	33	21	27	21	19
1944 Mar.	26		43	37	35	40	33	33	34	21	28	21	20
Nov.	27		43	40	37	40	33	33	35	22	29	22	21
1945 Mar.	29		45	40	38	43	34	34	37	23	31	23	21
Nov.	30		48	41	40	43	36	36	40	23	32	24	22
1946 Mar.	32		48	42	42	45	37	38	41	22	33	26	24
Nov.	34		49	44	45	47	40	41	44	23	36	27	26
1947 Mar.	36		52	47	49	47	41	42	47	25	36	30	28
Nov.	37		53	49	50	48	42	43	47	25	38	31	28
1948 Mar.	39		52	49	50	50	43	44	49	25	39	30	29
Nov.	41		54	52	54	52	46	44	51	26	40	31	30
1949 Mar.	41		55	50	54	51	45	44	52	27	41	31	30
Nov.	40		50	47	53	49	44	43	52	27	39	30	30

		U.S.[2]	Maine	N.H.	Vt.	Mass.	R.I.	Conn.	N.Y.	N.J.	Pa.	Del.	Md.
Date[1]								Northeast					
1950	Mar.	40	51	47	52	49	43	43	52	30	39	30	29
	Nov.	43	58	48	53	52	45	45	53	30	41	31	32
1951	Mar.	46	62	49	54	52	47	46	54	31	45	32	33
	Nov.	49	64	50	57	54	48	47	59	34	49	33	36
1952	Mar.	51	65	51	58	55	48	48	60	35	50	34	38
	Nov.	51	64	52	58	55	48	48	61	37	50	36	39
1953	Mar.	52	63	52	58	55	48	49	60	38	50	38	39
	Nov.	51	64	51	56	53	48	48	58	38	49	30	41
1954	Mar.	51	65	51	55	52	47	48	56	38	50	41	42
	Nov.	52	65	50	54	52	47	48	59	41	51	42	43
1955	Mar.	53	64	51	53	52	46	48	59	42	52	43	43
	Nov.	54	65	53	55	52	48	49	60	43	55	43	45
1956	Mar.	55	65	52	55	53	48	50	61	44	56	44	46
	Nov.	57	66	54	57	55	52	53	62	47	57	47	48
1957	Mar.	58	66	55	57	58	53	55	66	48	59	48	49
	Nov.	60	69	57	60	60	56	59	67	50	62	52	53
1958	Mar.	61	71	58	61	62	57	60	67	51	63	54	55
	Nov.	64	75	61	65	66	61	64	71	54	66	57	57
1959	Mar.	66	77	63	66	67	63	65	73	55	67	59	58
	Nov.	68	78	67	71	71	67	67	74	57	69	62	60
1960	Mar.	68	79	66	70	72	67	68	73	58	70	63	61
	Nov.	69	84	68	70	74	71	70	63	62	70	70	63
1961	Mar.	69	84	70	71	75	72	71	73	68	72	74	64
	Nov.	71	84	73	72	77	74	73	73	68	74	78	64
1962	Mar.	73	85	74	74	79	76	74	74	69	76	80	69
	Nov.	75	88	77	76	81	79	77	79	69	78	79	74
1963	Mar.	77	91	78	76	82	81	78	78	69	81	78	68
	Nov.	80	91	81	77	84	84	81	78	78	83	82	77
1964	Mar.	82	91	82	80	86	85	82	82	80	82	88	76
	Nov.	85	90	85	80	87	88	85	85	81	87	90	83
1965	Mar.	86	89	86	83	89	89	87	90	82	88	92	85
	Nov.	90	93	89	87	92	92	90	95	90	90	91	89
1966	Mar.	93	92	92	90	94	93	91	93	96	94	92	93
	Nov.	98	95	97	95	99	98	97	96	98	101	97	97
1967	Mar.	100	100	100	100	100	100	100	100	100	100	100	100
	Nov.	105	103	107	109	105	107	106	103	107	107	101	110
1968	Mar.	107	107	111	115	108	110	109	108	113	106	103	112
	Nov.	111	115	123	127	113	117	117	125	123	112	105	117
1969	Mar.	113	120	128	133	117	120	121	114	130	123	107	125
	Nov.	116	124	142	147	123	129	129	120	139	133	114	132
1970	Mar.	117	128	149	155	126	132	134	123	144	145	116	138
	Nov.	120	140	168	169	135	140	143	129	148	150	126	143
1971	Mar.	122	146	178	177	139	145	149	132	155	154	131	150
	Nov.	127	160	199	192	149	155	160	150	172	163	133	161
1972	Mar.	132			174[3]				155	180	167	134	162
	Nov.	141			187[3]				167	194	173	144	166

FARM REAL ESTATE (Cont.)

Date[1]		Lake States			Corn Belt					Northern Plains			
		Mich.	Wis.	Minn.	Ohio	Ind.	Ill.	Iowa	Mo.	N. Dak.	S. Dak.	Nebr.	Kans.
1912		20	35	27	24	21	25	30	30	33	49	35	28
1913		20	36	28	24	22	26	31	31	34	52	35	28
1914		21	37	29	25	23	27	32	32	35	52	36	28
1915		21	38	30	26	22	27	35	31	35	52	36	29
1916		23	43	34	27	24	27	39	33	39	55	37	30
1917		25	45	38	29	26	29	41	35	41	59	39	32
1918		27	48	43	32	28	31	45	39	43	64	45	34
1919		28	52	46	33	30	34	50	42	45	74	51	37
1920		32	62	59	38	36	42	66	51	50	92	63	42
1921		31	61	59	32	33	40	61	48	49	88	59	42
1922		30	56	52	30	26	33	50	41	47	75	51	36
1923		30	53	49	29	25	32	48	39	44	64	49	35
1924		28	50	47	29	24	30	44	36	39	60	45	33
1925		27	47	44	26	22	30	42	35	38	58	44	32
1926		26	45	43	25	21	29	40	32	36	55	43	31
1927		26	44	40	24	19	26	37	31	34	50	42	32
1928		26	43	39	23	18	25	36	30	34	49	41	31
1929		25	43	38	23	18	25	36	29	34	48	41	31
1930		25	42	37	22	18	24	35	28	33	47	40	31
1931		24	38	32	20	16	21	30	25	29	42	37	29
1932		20	33	27	17	13	17	25	21	25	34	32	25
1933		16	29	22	14	12	14	18	17	23	28	25	20
1934		17	29	23	15	12	15	20	18	23	28	25	20
1935		17	30	23	16	13	16	21	18	23	28	25	21
1936		17	31	24	17	15	17	22	18	24	28	26	21
1937		19	32	24	18	16	18	23	19	23	28	25	22
1938		19	32	24	18	16	19	23	18	22	26	24	22
1939		19	31	24	18	16	19	23	18	20	23	23	21
1940		19	30	24	19	16	20	23	18	18	21	21	20
1941		19	30	24	19	17	20	23	19	18	20	19	20
1942	Mar.	21	32	25	21	19	23	25	20	19	21	21	21
	Nov.	21	31	25	22	20	23	25	21	18	22	21	21
1943	Mar.	24	33	28	24	22	24	27	23	20	24	23	24
	Nov.	25	34	29	24	23	25	29	23	21	25	23	24
1944	Mar.	27	37	31	27	25	27	31	25	24	29	27	27
	Nov.	29	37	32	28	26	29	32	26	25	29	28	28
1945	Mar.	30	40	32	29	27	29	33	28	26	31	30	31
	Nov.	30	41	34	30	29	30	35	28	28	32	31	32
1946	Mar.	34	43	36	34	32	32	37	32	29	34	34	34
	Nov.	36	46	38	35	33	34	39	33	30	36	37	36
1947	Mar.	40	49	40	38	35	37	41	35	32	38	38	39
	Nov.	39	49	42	38	35	38	43	34	36	42	41	41
1948	Mar.	40	53	44	40	38	39	46	36	38	46	45	46
	Nov.	42	55	46	42	39	41	47	37	39	49	49	48
1949	Mar.	41	55	46	42	39	41	48	38	41	49	49	48
	Nov.	40	53	46	40	38	41	48	37	39	48	45	46

Date[1]		Lake States			Corn Belt					Northern Plains			
		Mich.	Wis.	Minn.	Ohio	Ind.	Ill.	Iowa	Mo.	N. Dak.	S. Dak.	Nebr.	Kans.
1950	Mar.	41	53	47	40	38	42	49	38	40	49	46	47
	Nov.	43	55	51	45	43	47	52	41	41	51	49	50
1951	Mar.	47	59	54	48	46	50	56	45	43	53	53	53
	Nov.	48	62	58	51	49	52	59	48	46	57	57	55
1952	Mar.	50	62	59	54	50	54	60	50	49	60	59	58
	Nov.	51	62	60	54	51	55	59	50	49	60	60	58
1953	Mar.	52	63	60	54	52	55	58	50	52	60	62	59
	Nov.	52	61	57	54	50	56	57	48	51	59	60	58
1954	Mar.	52	60	57	55	51	56	57	48	51	58	58	58
	Nov.	53	59	59	57	53	57	59	49	50	59	60	59
1955	Mar.	55	60	59	58	54	57	60	49	51	60	61	60
	Nov.	56	62	64	61	56	59	61	51	52	60	61	61
1956	Mar.	58	63	64	62	57	60	61	51	52	60	60	62
	Nov.	60	66	66	65	60	63	63	53	55	61	59	63
1957	Mar.	62	67	68	66	61	65	64	54	57	62	59	64
	Nov.	64	69	72	68	63	65	66	57	59	65	61	66
1958	Mar.	64	70	75	69	64	66	66	58	61	67	63	67
	Nov.	67	73	77	71	66	69	69	60	64	71	66	60
1959	Mar.	71	76	79	72	67	71	71	62	67	73	67	71
	Nov.	72	76	80	72	69	71	72	62	67	73	69	72
1960	Mar.	72	76	80	73	69	71	73	63	69	74	69	72
	Nov.	72	76	77	72	66	70	71	64	69	74	69	72
1961	Mar.	73	78	78	72	66	69	69	65	71	74	70	72
	Nov.	75	79	80	73	66	70	70	68	73	76	71	74
1962	Mar.	76	81	82	75	68	71	72	68	73	79	75	75
	Nov.	77	83	81	77	69	73	72	69	75	80	77	78
1963	Mar.	78	80	84	77	71	75	73	70	80	84	75	78
	Nov.	79	79	86	79	73	77	74	75	83	84	78	80
1964	Mar.	81	84	86	83	76	78	76	77	83	85	81	82
	Nov.	83	86	88	85	81	82	78	80	87	85	83	86
1965	Mar.	84	85	90	86	80	84	79	82	87	86	86	88
	Nov.	88	87	93	90	83	88	84	83	90	89	90	93
1966	Mar.	89	91	94	93	92	94	89	89	93	94	92	95
	Nov.	93	95	99	99	98	101	96	97	97	97	99	100
1967	Mar.	100	100	100	100	100	100	100	100	100	100	100	100
	Nov.	105	105	104	105	106	104	103	108	105	105	105	103
1968	Mar.	103	104	107	106	106	104	105	109	108	106	108	107
	Nov.	109	112	113	109	108	106	111	114	113	107	113	111
1969	Mar.	110	114	112	110	106	109	111	119	117	108	113	110
	Nov.	113	122	115	114	105	108	114	125	121	109	115	109
1970	Mar.	113	124	118	115	104	107	114	124	120	112	115	107
	Nov.	115	131	119	116	104	107	116	128	121	114	116	104
1971	Mar.	115	137	121	120	109	108	114	130	122	114	117	109
	Nov.	119	142	124	123	113	110	116	136	125	117	120	111
1972	Mar.	127	148	127	127	113	116	122	143	127	118	127	118
	Nov.	135	162	136	137	119	124	130	157	134	122	137	129

FARM REAL ESTATE (Cont.)

Date[1]		Appalachian					Southeast				Delta States		
		Va.	W. Va.	N.C.	Ky.	Tenn.	S.C.	Ga.	Fla.	Ala.	Miss.	Ark.	La.
1912		16	30	12	16	16	19	14	12	12	11	12	14
1913		16	31	12	16	16	19	15	12	12	12	12	15
1914		17	32	13	17	17	19	15	13	12	12	12	14
1915		16	31	13	16	16	18	13	12	12	11	11	14
1916		19	32	14	18	18	19	15	13	12	13	13	15
1917		20	35	16	21	20	21	17	14	12	14	16	16
1918		23	38	19	24	24	23	19	16	15	15	18	21
1919		27	42	22	28	27	31	25	18	17	18	20	23
1920		31	48	28	32	33	44	31	22	21	25	27	28
1921		29	44	24	28	28	36	25	22	18	17	22	23
1922		26	39	21	24	25	24	20	20	16	17	21	20
1923		28	40	24	24	26	25	18	19	17	17	20	21
1924		26	39	24	23	24	26	18	20	17	16	19	20
1925		25	37	23	23	22	27	17	22	18	16	19	20
1926		24	36	23	23	22	24	16	28	18	16	18	21
1927		22	34	22	22	21	22	15	23	17	15	18	19
1928		22	34	21	21	21	21	15	22	17	14	18	19
1929		22	33	20	21	20	21	15	22	17	14	17	19
1930		22	33	20	21	20	20	14	22	17	14	17	19
1931		19	31	17	19	19	17	13	21	16	13	14	17
1932		16	25	14	16	16	14	10	18	12	11	12	15
1933		14	23	11	13	13	11	8	15	11	8	10	13
1934		15	24	13	13	14	13	9	16	12	10	10	14
1935		16	24	14	14	15	15	10	16	13	11	11	15
1936		17	25	15	14	16	15	10	16	14	11	11	15
1937		18	26	16	16	16	16	11	17	14	11	11	16
1938		18	26	17	17	17	17	11	17	15	12	12	17
1939		18	27	17	17	17	17	12	16	15	12	11	17
1940		18	27	17	18	18	17	12	17	15	12	11	17
1941		19	28	17	18	19	18	13	17	15	13	12	17
1942	Mar.	19	28	19	21	20	20	13	19	16	14	13	18
	Nov.	21	29	20	21	21	21	13	20	15	14	14	19
1943	Mar.	21	31	20	24	23	22	15	21	17	16	15	21
	Nov.	22	31	21	25	24	23	16	23	17	16	16	21
1944	Mar.	24	33	24	27	26	26	17	24	19	17	17	22
	Nov.	25	33	25	27	26	27	17	26	20	17	17	22
1945	Mar.	28	33	28	30	29	31	19	28	21	19	20	23
	Nov.	29	35	29	32	31	32	20	31	22	20	21	24
1946	Mar.	32	38	33	35	35	33	21	34	25	23	21	25
	Nov.	34	40	35	38	36	35	23	33	26	24	23	27
1947	Mar.	36	43	38	42	40	37	25	32	30	25	25	29
	Nov.	36	43	38	43	40	37	25	30	29	25	27	29
1948	Mar.	37	46	40	42	42	40	26	28	30	27	28	29
	Nov.	40	48	41	44	42	42	28	28	31	28	31	32
1949	Mar.	40	48	42	45	44	43	28	28	33	29	31	33
	Nov.	39	43	42	43	43	39	26	27	31	28	29	32

		Appalachian					Southeast				Delta States		
Date[1]		Va.	W. Va.	N.C.	Ky.	Tenn.	S.C.	Ga.	Fla.	Ala.	Miss.	Ark.	La.
1950	Mar.	38	43	42	44	43	39	26	28	31	29	30	32
	Nov.	42	44	45	48	46	41	28	31	33	31	31	33
1951	Mar.	44	48	47	50	48	43	29	32	35	33	36	34
	Nov.	47	50	49	54	51	45	32	34	37	35	38	35
1952	Mar.	49	51	53	56	52	47	34	35	39	36	39	36
	Nov.	50	50	55	54	52	49	35	36	40	37	40	39
1953	Mar.	50	50	56	54	52	49	36	36	41	37	40	40
	Nov.	49	49	56	53	49	50	35	38	40	36	39	42
1954	Mar.	49	50	56	52	49	51	35	39	39	36	39	43
	Nov.	51	50	58	53	50	52	36	41	41	36	39	44
1955	Mar.	52	50	58	54	51	53	37	41	43	36	40	44
	Nov.	54	52	59	54	52	55	38	43	44	40	42	45
1956	Mar.	55	53	59	55	53	56	39	46	46	42	43	46
	Nov.	57	55	62	58	54	57	42	51	47	46	44	49
1957	Mar.	58	56	63	59	55	58	42	54	47	47	45	51
	Nov.	60	59	64	62	56	59	45	58	49	48	47	55
1958	Mar.	61	60	65	63	57	60	46	62	50	49	48	56
	Nov.	64	63	67	66	60	62	49	67	53	51	48	61
1959	Mar.	66	65	68	68	63	64	51	72	55	52	49	63
	Nov.	67	66	69	70	65	66	54	74	56	53	53	65
1960	Mar.	67	66	69	71	66	68	55	74	57	53	54	66
	Nov.	68	70	69	71	67	68	55	77	58	54	54	65
1961	Mar.	70	73	71	72	68	68	56	77	63	55	54	63
	Nov.	71	73	75	73	71	70	58	80	65	60	57	67
1962	Mar.	76	77	81	77	72	73	60	82	62	62	59	67
	Nov.	78	82	82	82	74	75	64	86	65	61	65	70
1963	Mar.	76	82	84	83	79	76	62	88	71	64	68	72
	Nov.	81	85	87	86	82	77	66	92	79	68	75	78
1964	Mar.	80	89	86	88	83	81	70	94	76	74	79	81
	Nov.	81	94	90	91	86	83	75	98	78	80	82	80
1965	Mar.	85	93	91	93	88	88	80	100	85	81	84	80
	Nov.	89	90	94	92	95	96	85	100	93	88	91	86
1966	Mar.	95	96	93	88	96	95	88	101	92	95	96	88
	Nov.	101	100	99	92	100	99	94	102	99	98	99	90
1967	Mar.	100	100	100	100	100	100	100	100	100	100	100	100
	Nov.	105	105	105	109	101	105	103	101	103	107	108	105
1968	Mar.	107	114	108	108	109	110	108	105	112	108	113	105
	Nov.	108	123	112	110	113	122	120	107	120	110	119	108
1969	Mar.	110	124	116	111	117	125	126	109	117	118	123	110
	Nov.	116	133	115	117	119	125	137	114	123	122	126	113
1970	Mar.	121	137	113	116	123	124	138	121	121	125	129	116
	Nov.	131	147	120	117	127	132	146	122	131	125	128	122
1971	Mar.	132	153	128	123	128	135	152	128	139	127	127	127
	Nov.	140	166	136	129	130	144	161	130	143	128	137	133
1972	Mar.	149	177	138	137	142	162	175	136	146	129	143	139
	Nov.	160	194	154	146	156	173	195	[4]	154	134	148	146

FARM REAL ESTATE (Cont.)

Date[1]		Southern Plains		Mountain								Pacific		
		Okla.	Tex.	Mont.	Idaho	Wyo.	Colo.	N. Mex.	Ariz.	Utah	Nev.	Wash.	Oreg.	Calif.
1912		17	19	25	20	19	28	19	13	29	29	21	19	15
1913		18	20	26	20	21	30	20	13	29	30	21	19	16
1914		18	21	27	19	20	28	18	14	28	31	22	20	18
1915		17	20	26	19	21	27	19	13	28	31	21	19	18
1916		18	20	25	19	19	29	18	13	30	30	22	19	19
1917		20	23	26	22	19	31	21	14	34	29	24	20	21
1918		23	26	28	26	24	32	22	17	35	31	25	22	22
1919		25	28	30	28	29	34	24	19	42	35	26	23	23
1920		29	34	33	34	35	41	27	22	48	41	30	25	27
1921		28	31	27	32	29	38	23	20	39	37	29	25	28
1922		25	26	25	27	27	35	22	18	38	36	27	23	27
1923		23	25	23	26	24	33	21	17	38	34	25	22	27
1924		22	27	21	25	22	28	21	17	38	32	25	22	27
1925		23	29	20	24	20	27	20	16	38	31	24	21	27
1926		23	29	19	23	19	26	20	17	37	30	24	21	27
1927		23	28	20	24	19	26	20	17	38	30	25	21	27
1928		23	27	21	25	20	26	20	18	38	30	24	21	27
1929		22	27	22	26	22	26	20	18	38	30	24	21	27
1930		22	27	21	25	22	26	21	18	36	30	24	21	27
1931		21	24	19	22	21	24	20	17	32	27	21	19	25
1932		17	19	15	18	16	18	16	13	28	23	18	15	20
1933		13	16	12	14	12	14	13	10	23	18	15	12	15
1934		15	17	13	15	12	14	13	10	23	18	16	12	15
1935		15	18	13	16	12	14	14	11	23	18	17	12	16
1936		16	19	14	16	13	15	14	12	23	19	18	13	17
1937		16	19	14	18	14	16	14	13	24	20	20	14	19
1938		17	19	14	18	14	16	15	12	23	20	20	14	18
1939		17	19	14	18	14	16	15	12	23	20	20	14	17
1940		16	19	14	18	15	17	15	12	23	20	20	14	16
1941		17	19	15	18	15	17	16	13	25	20	21	15	16
1942	Mar.	18	21	16	20	17	19	17	14	27	22	23	16	18
	Nov.	17	21	16	22	18	21	20	16	28	22	24	17	19
1943	Mar.	20	22	18	23	19	21	20	17	29	24	26	18	21
	Nov.	20	22	19	26	21	23	24	18	31	27	28	20	24
1944	Mar.	21	24	21	28	22	25	25	20	33	29	31	22	26
	Nov.	22	26	23	30	23	28	27	21	35	31	32	24	30
1945	Mar.	23	27	23	32	25	29	29	22	35	33	34	25	31
	Nov.	24	29	25	34	27	33	32	24	39	35	37	27	35
1946	Mar.	27	30	26	35	29	34	33	26	40	37	39	30	36
	Nov.	29	32	29	39	32	40	36	28	45	40	43	33	39
1947	Mar.	30	33	31	39	33	41	37	29	45	40	43	33	39
	Nov.	31	35	33	42	36	44	40	30	49	41	45	35	39
1948	Mar.	33	37	33	43	39	45	42	30	49	41	46	35	39
	Nov.	36	40	37	46	40	47	44	31	53	42	48	38	38
1949	Mar.	37	37	36	44	38	48	44	30	50	40	46	34	37
	Nov.	35	35	35	45	37	47	44	30	51	40	45	34	36

[1] Index values are as of March 1 unless specified otherwise.
[2] Excludes Alaska and Hawaii; excludes Florida after March 1972.
[3] Weighted average of indexes for Maine, N.H., Vt., Mass., R.I., and Conn.

Date[1]		Southern Plains		Mountain								Pacific		
		Okla.	Tex.	Mont.	Idaho	Wyo.	Colo.	N. Mex.	Ariz.	Utah	Nev.	Wash.	Oreg.	Calif.
1950	Mar.	36	36	35	45	37	46	44	29	52	40	45	34	36
	Nov.	40	40	38	48	44	51	46	31	57	44	50	36	41
1951	Mar.	42	44	42	53	43	54	50	33	59	46	52	39	42
	Nov.	45	46	46	56	45	59	56	37	64	50	57	40	46
1952	Mar.	46	49	47	57	47	59	56	37	65	52	57	41	47
	Nov.	45	49	48	59	47	59	56	40	66	52	59	43	48
1953	Mar.	44	49	48	58	47	58	56	40	66	51	60	43	48
	Nov.	44	49	47	57	45	56	54	39	64	53	59	42	47
1954	Mar.	44	50	47	57	45	57	55	40	64	55	59	42	47
	Nov.	47	51	47	59	45	56	55	41	66	56	61	43	49
1955	Mar.	48	52	49	60	45	57	56	41	66	56	61	43	49
	Nov.	48	52	52	62	46	58	56	42	66	57	65	45	51
1956	Mar.	49	52	53	63	47	57	56	43	68	58	64	45	53
	Nov.	49	55	55	63	49	58	55	45	69	60	65	46	56
1957	Mar.	50	57	56	65	49	59	55	47	71	60	66	47	57
	Nov.	52	55	59	67	53	62	57	49	73	62	68	49	60
1958	Mar.	52	55	60	68	54	63	57	50	73	62	68	49	62
	Nov.	55	58	65	71	57	65	57	52	74	63	70	50	66
1959	Mar.	57	59	67	73	60	66	59	53	77	64	70	51	68
	Nov.	60	64	70	75	60	68	61	56	80	66	72	52	71
1960	Mar.	61	67	71	76	62	69	62	56	80	67	73	52	72
	Nov.	61	68	71	75	66	69	63	59	81	69	74	57	76
1961	Mar.	61	69	71	75	70	70	62	61	82	70	76	63	77
	Nov.	62	71	74	75	75	76	66	65	83	72	78	64	80
1962	Mar.	68	72	77	78	76	78	69	67	84	73	75	65	80
	Nov.	73	74	80	81	78	81	72	69	85	74	74	71	84
1963	Mar.	73	76	80	81	79	83	74	71	86	75	81	74	85
	Nov.	77	81	80	87	77	84	80	75	86	77	85	78	88
1964	Mar.	80	87	84	84	74	89	83	78	86	78	86	79	89
	Nov.	82	88	88	87	82	88	86	84	86	81	88	87	90
1965	Mar.	87	89	89	91	88	88	88	85	89	83	88	91	91
	Nov.	93	93	94	94	88	94	93	90	92	88	91	93	93
1966	Mar.	93	97	97	93	88	97	95	93	94	90	93	95	94
	Nov.	98	99	100	98	99	98	98	97	97	97	97	98	97
1967	Mar.	100	100	100	100	100	100	100	100	100	100	100	100	100
	Nov.	105	103	102	105	101	101	104	104	105	109	108	104	103
1968	Mar.	108	109	107	109	102	100	106	106	108	114	114	107	105
	Nov.	110	113	109	112	97	104	110	110	118	126	119	115	109
1969	Mar.	108	114	111	116	102	105	112	115	122	132	121	120	109
	Nov.	115	118	119	120	113	105	118	123	131	147	123	131	109
1970	Mar.	115	119	124	120	116	105	120	127	137	155	124	137	110
	Nov.	115	122	129	124	121	110	125	136	148	171	123	146	109
1971	Mar.	122	125	131	128	119	114	127	139	154	181	124	152	109
	Nov.	128	129	136	138	132	121	132	149	165	200	127	163	111
1972	Mar.	131	138	142	141	134	128	136	159	173	213	130	170	112
	Nov.	138	147	148	150	139	134	143	164	180	238	133	179	113

[4] Insufficient data for publication.
Source: Economic Research Service, U.S. Department of Agriculture.

FARM REAL ESTATE VALUES

Average Value per Acre, by State, Grouped by
Farm Production Region, March 1, 1970–74

State	1970	1971	1972	1973	1974
Northeast					
[1] Maine	$ 161	$ 183	$ 206	$ 235	$ 276
[1] New Hampshire	239	287	323	368	432
[1] Vermont	224	256	288	328	385
[1] Massachusetts	565	623	702	799	939
[1] Rhode Island	734	807	910	1,036	1,217
[1] Connecticut	921	1,025	1,155	1,316	1,546
New York	273	292	344	390	516
New Jersey	1,092	1,171	1,364	1,599	2,099
Pennsylvania	373	396	430	518	675
Delaware	499	559	574	663	851
Maryland	640	699	752	888	1,056
Lake States					
Michigan	326	331	366	433	503
Wisconsin	232	257	278	336	401
Minnesota	226	231	243	275	354
Corn Belt					
Ohio	399	413	438	507	636
Indiana	406	426	441	512	629
Illinois	490	491	527	590	788
Iowa	392	392	418	482	648
Missouri	224	236	259	289	374
Northern Plains					
North Dakota	94	96	99	111	151
South Dakota	84	85	89	97	129
Nebraska	154	157	171	195	246
Kansas	159	161	176	203	265
Appalachian					
Virginia	286	312	352	404	528
West Virginia	136	151	175	208	271
North Carolina	333	378	407	483	589
Kentucky	253	268	297	333	394
Tennessee	268	279	311	363	449

[1] The average rate of change for the six New England States was used to project dollar values for each of these six states for 1972–74.
[2] Revised May 1974.

State	1970	1971	1972	1973	1974
Southeast					
South Carolina	261	284	341	375	501
Georgia	234	258	297	340	448
Florida	355	376	398	454[2,3]	586[3]
Alabama	200	229	239	274	347
Delta States					
Mississippi	$204	$239	$242	$269	$342
Arkansas	260	257	288	321	376
Louisiana	321	352	386	411	483
Southern Plains					
Oklahoma	173	183	197	225	275
Texas	148	155	172	194	238
Mountain					
Montana	60	63	68	76	97
Idaho	177	189	208	234	298
Wyoming	41	42	47	54	67
Colorado	95	103	110	138	176
New Mexico	42	44	47	53	65
Arizona	70	76	87	93	114
Utah	92	103	115	124	145
Nevada	53	63	73	87	103
Pacific					
Washington	224	225	234	262	290
Oregon	150	166	185	204	233
California	475	471	485	496	566
48 States	195	203	219	247	310

[3] Estimated by the average of the percentage change in Georgia and Alabama index values.
Source: Economic Research Service, U.S. Department of Agriculture.

FARM REAL ESTATE

Indexes of Average Value per Acre, by State, Grouped by Farm
Production Region, 1960, 1965, and 1970–74[1]
(1967 = 100)

State	1960	1965	1970	1971	1972	1973	1974
Northeast							
Maine	79	89	128	146			
New Hampshire	66	86	149	178			
Vermont	70	83	155	177	174	198	232
Massachusetts	72	89	126	139			
Rhode Island	67	89	132	145			
Connecticut	68	87	134	149			
New York	73	90	123	132	155	176	233
New Jersey	58	82	144	155	180	211	278
Pennsylvania	70	88	145	154	167	201	262
Delaware	63	92	116	131	134	155	199
Maryland	61	85	138	150	162	191	227
Lake States							
Michigan	72	84	113	115	127	150	174
Wisconsin	76	85	124	137	148	179	214
Minnesota	80	90	118	121	127	144	186
Corn Belt							
Ohio	73	86	115	120	127	147	184
Indiana	69	80	104	109	113	131	161
Illinois	71	84	107	108	116	129	173
Iowa	73	79	114	114	122	141	189
Missouri	63	82	124	130	143	160	207
Northern Plains							
North Dakota	69	87	120	122	127	142	193
South Dakota	74	86	112	114	118	130	172
Nebraska	69	86	115	117	127	145	183
Kansas	72	88	107	109	118	137	178
Appalachian							
Virginia	67	85	121	132	149	171	223
West Virginia	66	93	137	153	177	211	275
North Carolina	69	91	113	128	138	164	200
Kentucky	71	93	116	123	137	153	182
Tennessee	66	88	123	128	142	167	206

[1] March 1 values. Includes improvements.
[2] Estimated by the average of the percentage change in Georgia and Alabama index values.

State	1960	1965	1970	1971	1972	1973	1974
Southeast							
South Carolina	68	88	124	135	162	179	238
Georgia	55	80	138	152	175	201	264
Florida	74	100	121	128	136	155[2]	200[2]
Alabama	57	85	121	139	146	167	211
Delta States							
Mississippi	53	81	125	127	129	144	182
Arkansas	54	84	129	127	143	159	186
Louisiana	66	80	116	127	139	148	174
Southern Plains							
Oklahoma	61	87	115	122	131	150	183
Texas	67	89	119	125	130	158	191
Mountain							
Montana	71	89	124	131	142	159	203
Idaho	76	91	120	128	141	159	203
Wyoming	62	88	116	119	134	153	191
Colorado	69	88	105	114	128	152	194
New Mexico	62	88	120	127	136	151	186
Arizona	56	85	127	139	159	170	208
Utah	80	89	137	154	173	186	216
Nevada	67	83	155	181	213	251	299
Pacific							
Washington	73	88	124	124	130	145	160
Oregon	52	91	137	152	170	187	213
California	72	91	110	109	112	115	131
48 States	68	86	117	122	132	150	187

Source: Economic Research Service, U.S. Department of Agriculture.

61 Useful lives of buildings

How many years will a building have value?

Many guidelines are available.

A classic observation is that far more buildings are torn down than fall down.

With routine maintenance, buildings may stand for centuries. However, the salient question is not how long a building *could* stand but how long it *should* stand. The answer is likely to depend more on design factors and location factors than on physical factors.

This is one way to view a building's probable useful life: How long is this building likely to add significant value to the site?

Another way to look at the same thing: Over what period of years would a prudent investor require recapture of his investment in this building?

Some of the more noteworthy guidelines may be summarized as follows:

1. In 1942, the Treasury issued *Bulletin F, Tables of Useful Lives of Depreciable Property.** For new buildings which are to be depreciated on a composite (or overall) basis, the depreciation rates set out in *Bulletin F* were apparently based upon these useful lives:

Type of building	Type of construction		
	Good	Average	Cheap
Apartment	40 years	40 years	33 years
Bank	50	50	40
Dwelling	50	40	33
Factory	44	40	33
Farm	50	50	40
Garage	50	40	33
Grain elevator	67	50	40
Hotel	40	40	33
Loft	50	50	33
Machine shop	50	40	33
Office	50	40	33
Store	50	50	40
Theater	40	33	29
Warehouse	67	50	40

* Treasury Department, Internal Revenue Service, Publication No. 173.

However, for buildings to be depreciated on a component basis, *Bulletin F* sets out these guidelines for the shells (*new*). . .

Type of building	Years of life
Apartment	50
Bank	67
Dwelling	60
Factory	50
Farm	60
Garage	60
Grain elevator	75
Hotel	50
Loft	67
Machine shop	60
Office	67
Store	67
Theater	50
Warehouse	75

And the guidelines for various other components (*new*):

Item	Useful life
Air-Conditioning Systems:	
Large (over 20 tons)	20 years
Medium (5 to 15 tons)	15
Small (under 5 tons)	10
Elevators:	
Freight	25
Passenger	20
Heating Systems:	
Boilers and furnaces	20
Radiators	25
Gas-burner equipment	16
Oil-burner equipment	10
Lighting Systems:	
Fixtures	15
Wiring	20
Plumbing Systems:	
Faucets and valves	15–20

Fixtures (tubs, bowls, etc.)	25
Iron cold-water pipes	25
Iron hot-water or steam pipes	20
Roofs:	
Asbestos	25
Asphalt and tar	15
Galvanized iron	15–20
Tar and gravel (5-ply)	20
Tarred felt	10
Wells and Well Pumps	25
Miscellaneous:	
Awnings	5
Louver (ventilating) doors	15
Incinerators	14
Window screens	10

Even though no convincing showing was ever made that these useful lives were accurate or truly representative, they came to be accepted as such by many.

2. In 1962, the Treasury set out these alternative guidlines* for *new* improvements:

Type of improvements	Useful life
Land improvements (including paving, sewers, sidewalks, landscaping, shrubbery, and all fences except farm fences. Excludes golf course and cemetery improvements)	20 years
Apartment buildings	40
Bank buildings	50
Dwellings	45
Factories	45
Garages	45
Grain elevators	60
Hotels	40
Loft buildings	50
Machine shops	45
Office buildings	45
Stores	50
Theaters	40
Warehouses	60
Farm buildings	25
Furnishings in hotels, motels, offices	10

* *Depreciation Guidelines and Rules,* U.S. Treasury Department, Internal Revenue Service, Publication No. 456.

3. Often, an IRS director has made an agreement with a building owner as to the useful life of that building. Sometimes the useful lives agreed upon are revealed in financial statements.

4. Often, disagreements between IRS and building owners over useful lives are taken to court. The voluminous case law provides some very interesting guidelines (guidelines best interpreted by one's lawyer and accountant if they are to be used for income tax purposes).

5. Private studies have produced some much more persuasive guidelines.

   Example: An authoritative 1973 report on a cross section of shopping centers set out guidelines on depreciable lives (estimated 22–29 years). (*Depreciable Lives of Shopping Centers,* an Independent Study Prepared for the International Council of Shopping Centers by Touche Ross & Co.)

   Example: In its annual summary of operations on the motel industry, *Motel/Motor Inn Journal* reports on estimated useful lives assigned to motel buildings of various ages and sizes. The same median depreciable life (25 years) was noted eight years in a row.

6. Some cost manuals report typical useful lives, based partly upon how old various types of buildings are when they are razed or extensively remodeled.

7. Variations in life expectancy may be related to ownership or tenancy.

   Example: Lives of service stations owned by oil companies have typically been longer than those of stations leased from private parties.

   Example: In a recent tax court case, it was affirmed that the useful life of shopping center improvements may be related to the major tenant's lease term.

8. The most authoritative figure of all may be the one provided by a qualified and recognized expert (See Chapter 65) who has studied the property in question. Often, an unbiased expert is retained by a building owner to allocate the cost basis to various components and/or to render an opinion on useful life.

Well-informed real estate investors are interested in two concepts of useful life: (1) what period of years will IRS accept as the *depreciable* life, and (2) what period of years is the likely *economic* life? Often the two are about the same. Often they are not.

62

Depreciation tables

Depreciation tables are widely used.

They are not reliable reflections of the market.

More than 50 books—mostly building-cost manuals and guides for tax assessors—include depreciation tables akin to the accompanying sample.

The wide circulation and use of such tables is not too difficult to understand. If the cost approach is to be used in valuing a building, one necessary step is to estimate the amount of accrued depreciation, and this step can be a tough one for even the most able appraiser. Use of a depreciation table may seem like an easy way to dispose of that problem. Further, property insurance underwiters and real estate tax assessors are encouraged to use such tables to put "values" on a more consistent basis.

However, depreciation tables of this sort are unreliable. Objections include these:

1. That the tables represent typical rates of depreciation is not documented at all in most cases. (Since figures vary from one depreciation table to another, the first exercise of judgment may be needed in choosing a table.)

2. Typical useful lives vary substantially from one type of building to another. (A fireproof bank building may have a useful life two times—or even three times—that of a block and frame service station building.)

3. At best, such tables reflect average depreciation, and individual variations from the average can be—and often are—quite large. (Two chain store buildings with the same prototype plans and specifications can have markedly different useful lives because of differences in location factors.)

4. Design factors and location factors are not recognized *directly* in these tables. (House A is very similar to House B in design and construction. House A is younger and in better condition but has suffered far more depreciation, because House A is located near the end of a busy airport runway, while House B has a much better location.)

5. There is no tool native to the cost approach—that is, not borrowed from the market data approach or the income approach—that can measure some types of depreciation convincingly. (Say an apartment project is about 30 percent depreciated the day it is completed because its design is not appropriate in its submarket. This is a form of depreciation that *can* be reflected realistically and convincingly in the income approach, but *cannot* be with a table like this.)

6. Because of periodic updating (or any of several other factors), a structure's *effective age* may be quite different from its *physical age.*

7. Generally, the cost (less depreciation) approach is a very questionable approach to valuing a building when accrued depreciation represents a very large percentage of that building's reproduction cost. (Can the appraiser convincingly show that accrued depreciation is approximately 87 percent and not 80 or 95 percent? Perhaps he can, if he has enough data to do so *in one or both of the other two approaches to value.*)

Those who recommend the use of such tables often (quite properly) emphasize that these tables are only *guides,* and they encourage the reader to use judgment. To be sure, the reader *can* use his judgment to modify figures in a table to reflect individual differences in design, remodeling, location factors, and economic factors. However, the reader who possesses the experience and judgment to make appropriate allowances for all of these factors really has no need for the table.

AVERAGE PERCENTAGES
OF DEPRECIATION

	Observed condition of structure						Observed condition of structure				
Age	Very good	Good	Average	Poor	Very poor	Age	Very good	Good	Average	Poor	Very poor
1	1%	2%	3%	15%	30%	36	47%	50%	54%	64%	75%
2	1	3	4	16	30	37	48	51	55	65	76
3	2	4	6	17	30	38	49	52	56	67	78
4	2	5	7	18	30	39	49	53	57	68	79
5	3	6	8	19	31	40	50	54	58	69	81
6	4	7	9	20	32	41	51	55	59	70	82
7	6	8	11	22	33	42	51	55	60	71	83
8	7	10	13	23	34	43	52	56	61	72	84
9	8	11	14	24	35	44	52	57	62	73	85
10	10	13	16	26	36	45	52	57	63	74	85
11	12	14	17	27	37	46	53	58	63	75	87
12	13	16	19	29	39	47	54	59	64	76	87
13	15	17	20	30	40	48	54	59	65	77	88
14	16	19	22	32	42	49	55	60	66	78	89
15	18	20	23	33	43	50	55	61	67	79	90
16	19	22	25	35	45	51	55	61	68	79	90
17	21	23	26	36	46	52	56	62	69	80	91
18	22	25	28	38	48	53	57	63	70	81	92
19	24	26	29	39	49	54	57	64	71	82	93
20	25	28	31	41	51	55	58	65	72	83	94
21	27	29	32	42	52	56	58	65	73	84	95
22	28	31	34	44	54	57	59	66	74	85	96
23	30	32	35	45	55	58	60	67	75	86	97
24	31	34	37	47	57	59	61	68	76	87	98
25	33	35	38	48	58	60	61	69	77	88	99
26	34	37	40	50	60	61	62	70	78	89	100
27	36	38	41	51	61	62	63	71	79	89	100
28	37	40	43	53	63	63	63	72	80	90	100
29	39	41	44	54	64	64	64	73	81	90	100
30	40	43	46	56	66	65	64	73	82	91	100
31	42	44	47	57	67	66	65	74	82	91	100
32	43	46	49	59	69						
33	44	47	50	60	70						
34	45	48	52	62	72						
35	46	49	53	63	73						

 The CPI (Consumer Price Index)
as a tool for real estate people

The Consumer Price Index can be a useful tool for real estate professionals.

What does the Consumer Price Index have to do with real estate? Consider this example:

> In 1964, a landlord leased out his store for 20 years. The lease required the tenant to pay a flat $10,000 per year plus all expenses.

> If this lease had called for adjustments from time to time to reflect changes in the Consumer Price Index—*as thousands of leases now do*—the $10,000-per-year rent would have increased to more than $15,000 by 1974. Since it didn't, the landlord was still getting the same number of (shrinking) dollars each year—and he still had 10 years to go.

Though limited and flawed* and misunderstood, the Consumer Price Index is *the* most influential statistic coming out of Washington today. It is generally (but erroneously) accepted as an accurate gauge of inflation. In one way or another, the incomes of almost half the people in the country are tied to this one index.

If a rental-adjustment clause tied to the CPI is to be included in a lease (or other real estate agreement), don't forget to reach agreement on (1) which version of the CPI (national or city, seasonally adjusted or unadjusted, monthly or annual) you

* CPI is not a broad index. Its official name gives a clue to one of its most important limitations: "Consumer Price Index for Urban Earners and Clerical Workers." Well, urban wage earners and clerical workers and their families make up less than half the total population.

Further, CPI does *not* reflect how much families *actually spend*. It is often referred to as the cost-of-living index, but that's really *not* what it is.

What CPI does reflect is change in the cost of a "market basket" of 1960–61 goods and services, a "market basket" long out of date.

CPI does not include income taxes or other personal taxes.

In many cases, changes in prices are accompanied by changes in the *quality* of consumer goods and services.

CPI reflects only time-to-time changes in price in a given area. City indexes do not show differences in prices from place to place.

CPI does not reflect increased amounts of goods and services—most notably medical services—furnished to consumers at the cost of their employers.

CPI is not absolutely safe from bureaucratic tinkering. Reportedly, the cost of cigarettes was eliminated from the computations, not because people quit buying them but because some officials thought they *should*.

CPI reflects current interest rates on mortage loans even though only a fraction of consumers would be paying the new rates at any time.

The Bureau of Labor Statistics is working on a broader-based index which is scheduled to be unveiled in the spring of 1977. However, it is expected to continue issuing the current version of CPI as well.

want to use, (2) how often the rent will be adjusted and exactly how the adjustment will be computed, (3) whether rent will be reduced if the CPI goes down (it has happened), and (4) what will happen in the now-unlikely event the Bureau of Labor Statistics changes the composition of the CPI or stops publishing it.

One need not tie rental adjustment to the Consumer Price Index; other indexes or methods are available. For example, some prefer to use the Wholesale Price Index, and many prefer to use percentage-of-sales rental clauses. (See Chapter 55.)

Whatever method one chooses, inflation is a factor to be reckoned with in any long-term real estate agreement. The Red Queen could just as well have been talking about today's inflation when she told Alice, "It takes all the running you can do to keep in the same place. If you want to get somewhere else, you must run at least twice as fast as that!"

BRIEF EXPLANATION OF THE CPI

By the U.S. Department of Labor

The Consumer Price Index (CPI) measures average changes in prices of goods and services usually bought by urban wage earners and clerical workers. It is based on prices of about 400 items which were selected to represent the movement of prices of all goods and services purchased by wage earners and clerical workers. Prices for these items are obtained in urban portions of 39 major statistical areas and 17 smaller cities, which were chosen to represent all urban places in the United States. They are collected from about 18,000 establishments—grocery and department stores, hospitals, filling stations, and other types of stores and service establishments.

Prices of foods, fuels, and a few other items are obtained every month in all 56 locations. Prices of most other commodities and services are collected every month in the five largest areas and every 3 months in other areas. Prices of most goods and services are obtained by personal visits of the Bureau's trained representatives. Mail questionnaires are used to obtain local transit fares, public utility rates, newspaper prices, fuel prices, and certain other items.

In calculating the index, price changes for the various items in each location are averaged together with weights which represent their importance in the spending of all wage earners and clerical workers. Local data are then combined to obtain a U.S. city average. Separate indexes are also published for 23 areas.

The index measures price changes from a designated reference date—1967— which equals 100.0. An increase of 22 percent, for example, is shown as 122.0. This change can also be expressed in dollars as follows: The price of a base period "market basket" of goods and services bought by urban wage earners and clerical workers has risen from $10 in 1967 to $12.20.

CPI AND PURCHASING POWER OF CONSUMER DOLLAR OVER 40 YEARS

Year	Consumer Price Index (1967 = 100)	Purchasing power of the consumer dollar (1967 = $1.00)
1935	41.1	$2.433
1936	41.5	2.410
1937	43.0	2.326
1938	42.2	2.370
1939	41.6	2.392
1940	42.0	2.370
1941	44.1	2.160
1942	48.8	1.976
1943	51.8	1.916
1944	52.7	1.876
1945	53.9	1.835
1946	58.5	1.553
1947	66.9	1.425
1948	72.1	1.387
1949	71.4	1.412
1950	72.1	1.335
1951	77.8	1.261
1952	79.5	1.258
1953	80.1	1.248
1954	80.5	1.242
1955	80.2	1.247
1956	81.4	1.229
1957	84.3	1.186
1958	86.6	1.155
1959	87.3	1.145
1960	88.7	1.127
1961	89.6	1.116
1962	90.6	1.109
1963	91.7	1.091
1964	92.9	1.076
1965	94.5	1.058
1966	97.2	1.029
1967	100.0	1.000
1968	104.2	0.960
1969	109.8	0.911
1970	116.3	0.860
1971	121.3	0.824
1972	125.3	0.798
1973	133.1	0.751
1974	147.7	0.677

 **Developing your own rules of thumb**

Often, you can develop your own rule of thumb instead of relying on somebody else's.

Does an old rule of thumb really apply in a particular case?

If you have enough information to answer that question, you may be able to formulate a new rule of thumb or set of guidelines that will serve you better. As shown on the following examples, trying to find reasonable points of tendency in a particular submarket can (1) test the old "rules" and (2) focus on those elements which are most telling.

CASE NO. 1

Working for a major hotel chain, Ted Brown evaluates sites for new hotels.

For years, he has been aware of this rough rule of thumb for hotels: You can afford to invest $1,000 in land and improvements for each $1.25 to $1.50 of projected daily room rents.

Wanting preliminary checks on feasibility but unwilling to accept them blindly, Brown sets out to develop his own rule of thumb. He knows that the following figures are quite representative for new hotels in his chain:

   a. Room rentals are accounting for 60 percent of gross income.

   b. Occupancy is approximately 70 percent.

   c. Operating expenses are claiming 80 percent of the gross income actually received.

   d. A realistic overall capitalization rate for net income (before recapture and capital charges) is now 12 percent.

Using these figures:

$$\frac{(365 \text{ days @ } \$1.00/0.60) \ 0.70 \times 0.20}{0.12} = \$710$$

It was a simple matter for Brown to devise this rule of thumb: His chain can afford to invest roughly $710 for each $1.00 of potential daily room rentals.

As it turns out, Brown's "new" rule of thumb is quite consistent with the old $1.25–$1.50/$1,000 rule of thumb. ($1.00/$710 is equivalent to $1.41/$1,000) However, Brown has *tested* the "rule" and has developed a clearer fix on the component factors (which are likely to change from time to time).

CASE NO. 2

As the mortgage loan manager of a savings and loan association, Paul Green regularly reviews applications for loans on unfurnished garden-apartment projects in his city. Green knows that in the typical project:

    a. 5 percent of the rent roll is lost to vacancy.

    b. Operating expenses are claiming another 45 percent of the rent roll.

    c. Income from other (nonrental) sources is nominal.

    d. A fair overall rate of return is now on the order of 10 percent.

Using these figures . . .

$$\frac{\text{Each dollar of rent roll} \times 50\% \times 12 \text{ months}}{0.10}$$

. . . it's easy for Green to prepare this table which he uses to size up projects in a preliminary way:

Monthly rent per unit	Estimated value per unit
$125	$ 7,500
150	9,000
175	10,500
200	12,000
225	13,500
250	15,000
275	16,500
300	18,000
325	19,500
350	21,000
375	22,500
400	24,000

Green knows that this is just one of several preliminary checks and that it will not take the place of individual analysis and appraisal. However, this table helps Green spot wide variations from what he has found to be typical. (Sometimes these variations can be explained and justified.) Alternatively, Green could develop and use gross rent multiplers (in this case, a monthly GRM of 60 or annual GRM of 5).

 The best investment
in real estate

The best investment in real estate: The fee you pay for expert counsel.

Now, after all of this, here comes the author, unashamed and admitting to bias (indeed *insisting* on it) and telling you that bypassing independent research and advice to "save" time and money can be the costliest mistake in real estate.

Item: One of the largest shopping center developers has an outside firm checking market factors in every one of its centers on a regular basis.

Item: The largest fund investing in real estate is reported to have every property in its portfolio (worth hundreds of millions of dollars) appraised each year by an independent appraiser.

Item: Hundreds of mortgage lenders will not make final commitments without favorable advice from independent appraisers or consultants. Several require feasibility studies on large new projects.

Item: Real estate managers of many major corporations will not buy or sell a parcel without independent advice.

Item: Many developers request feasibility studies at an early stage in planning a new project.

Item: Property owners and their lawyers often refer real estate tax bills to qualified specialists to have them checked out for accuracy and fairness.

Why? In most cases, the answer is simple: Because it pays off.

A developer may hesitate to pay a $10,000-fee for a feasibility study on a $20 million shopping center, but this "saving" of *only one-twentieth of one percent* could be the riskiest kind of economy measure. Similarly, a prospective home buyer could "save" a $100 appraisal fee—just one-quarter of 1 percent of a $40,000 purchase price—and waste thousands.

How do you decide which real estate expert to retain? These points should be helpful:

1. Professional designations can tell you much about an individual's qualifications. However, as the reader can see in the summary at the end of this chapter, there are so many designations in the real estate field that they can be confusing as well.

   There are individuals without designations who can handle some types of real estate problems well, much as there are accountants without CPA designations who can handle some types of accounting problems well.

2. Some physicians are abler than others. The same is true of lawyers. And no two MAIs are created equal.

   One way to choose an expert is to find out who has been most successful in dealing with the sort of problem you have. Much as you might ask your family doctor to recommend a specialist, why not ask real estate professionals for the names of the most highly regarded real estate specialists.

3. Paying for more expertise than you need can be wasteful. However, if a serious doubt exists, its probably a good rule to retain the ablest expert you can find.

THREE OF THE MOST PRESTIGIOUS DESIGNATIONS IN REAL ESTATE

Designation	(Meaning)	Conferred by	Comments
CRE	(Counselor of Real Estate)	American Society of Real Estate Counselors 155 E. Superior St. Chicago, Ill. 60611	Each CRE was already well established as a real estate counselor before being invited to membership. Most already held an MAI designation, and several held other designations as well. In mid-1975, this select group numbered only approximately 429; stated another way, less than one-third of 1 percent of Realtors were CREs. A directory of CREs summarizes each member's areas of expertise.
MAI	(Member, Appraisal Institute)	American Institute of Real Estate Appraisers 155 E. Superior St. Chicago, Ill. 60611	This is believed by many to be the preferred designation in the area of appraising major income properties. An "MAI appraisal" is recognized as a "standard" in the field and is often specified in mortgage loan commitments and contracts of several types. There were approximately 3,912 MAIs —one out of every 34 or so Realtors—in mid-1975.
SREA	(Senior Real Estate Analyst)	Society of Real Estate Appraisers 7 S. Dearborn St. Chicago, Ill. 60603	This is the most complete professional endorsement that this large organization confers. SREAs, in addition to being skilled appraisers, have demonstrated abilities needed in solving advanced real estate problems. A unique requirement is that each designee must be recertified periodically. There were approximately 473 SREAs in mid-1975.

THE ALPHABET GAME

How to play: In the left-hand column are 26 of the designations (there are several more than this) in the real estate field. Cover the middle and right-hand columns and identify as many as you can. Par for professionals: 10 or more correct.

Designation	Meaning	Conferred by
AAE	Accredited Assessment Evaluator	International Association of Assessing Officers
AFLB	Accredited Farm and Land Broker	National Institute of Farm and Land Brokers
AFLM	Accredited Farm and Land Member	National Institute of Farm and Land Brokers
AFM	Accredited Farm Manager	American Society of Farm Managers and Rural Appraisers
AMO	Accredited Management Organization	Institute of Real Estate Management
ARA	Accredited Rural Appraiser	American Society of Farm Managers and Rural Appraisers
ASA	Senior Member	American Society of Appraisers
CAE	Certified Assessment Evaluator	International Association of Assessing Officers
CCIM	Certified Commercial Investment Member	National Institute of Real Estate Brokers
CPM	Certified Property Manager	Institute of Real Estate Management
CRB	Certified Residential Broker	National Institute of Real Estate Brokers
CRE	Counselor of Real Estate	American Society of Real Estate Counselors
CRSM	Certified Real Estate Securities Marketer	Real Estate Securities and Syndication Institute

* A popular misconception is that all licensed real estate brokers and salespeople are Realtors. In fact, a large percentage are not.

Designation	Meaning	Conferred by
CRSS	Certified Real Estate Securities Sponsor	Real Estate Securities and Syndication Institute
CSM	Certified Shopping Center Manager	International Council of Shopping Centers
GRI	Graduate, Realtor Institute	State associations related to National Association of Realtors
MAI	Member, Appraisal Institute	American Institute of Real Estate Appraisers
Realtor	Member	Local real estate board affiliated with National Association of Realtors*
RM	Residential Member	American Institute of Real Estate Appraisers
SIR	Member	Society of Industrial Realtors
SRA	Senior Residential Appraiser	Society of Real Estate Appraisers
SREA	Senior Real Estate Analyst	Society of Real Estate Appraisers
SRPA	Senior Real Property Appraiser	Society of Real Estate Appraisers
SR/WA	Senior Member	American Right of Way Association
AACI	Accredited Appraiser Canadian Institute	Appraisal Institute of Canada
CRA	Canadian Residential Appraiser	Appraisal Institute of Canada

Index

Apartments:
  best suited for conversion to condominiums, 88, 89
  debt coverage factors for, 122
  developing new rules of thumb for, 223
  FHA guidelines for, 28–34
  margins for conversion of, to condominiums, 87
  mortgage loan interest rates on, compared with other property types, 118
  parking requirements for, 43, 44
  sale prices of condominium units vs. value as, 85, 86
  typical operating ratios for, 150–152
  useful lives of, 210–213
Appraisers (*see* Designations, professional)
Assessed value as a guide to market value, 194

Band of Investment Method of selecting capitalization rates, 132, 133
Banks:
  locations for, 185–187
  percentage rents for, 172
  useful lives of, 210–213
Bond yields:
  compared with other rates, 124–126
  related to mortgage loan interest rates, 107–109
  use of, in Built-up Method, 130
Bowling centers:
  locations for, 187
  parking requirements for, 43, 44
  percentage rents for, 173, 176–181
  supportive population needed for, 50, 51
Brokers (*see* Designations, professional)
Buildings, useful lives of 210–213
Built-up Method of selecting capitalization rates, 130, 131

Capitalization rates:
  methods of selecting: Band of Investment Method, 132, 133
    Built-up Method, 130, 131
    Ellwood Method, 134

Capitalization rates, methods of selecting (*Cont.*):
    Gettel Method, 136–139
    Johnson Method, 134
    McLaughlin Method, 134
  mortgage-equity techniques, 134, 135
  proper, selection of, 128, 129
Car washes:
  percentage rents for, 172
  supportive population needed for, 50, 51
Cash flow, 104, 105
  sample projection of, 25
Churches:
  ideal maximum distances to, 38, 39
  parking requirements of, 43, 44
Condominiums:
  advantages of, 88–90
  best apartments for conversion to, 88, 89
  best time to buy, 91–93
  margins for conversions to, 87
  parking requirements for, 43, 44
  Rule of 100: New, 83, 84
    Old, 81, 82
  sale prices of, vs. value as apartments, 85, 86
Constants (*see* Percent constants)
Consultants (*see* Designations, professional)
Consumer Price Index (CPI), 217–220
Corner lot rules, 67–70
CRE (Counselor of Real Estate), 227
Cul-de-sacs, lots on, 68

Debt coverage factors:
  for major income properties, 121–123
  use of, in selecting capitalization rates, 136–139
Depreciation on useful lives of buildings, 210–213
Depreciation tables, 214–216
Depth rules for lots:
  4-3-2-1 Rule, 58, 59
  Hoffman-Neill Rule, 56, 57
  Hoffman Rule, 55
  others, 62
  parabolic formula, 60, 61
Designations, professional, 225–229

Distances, ideal maximum, to daily activities, 38, 39
Dwellings (*see* Houses)

Ellwood Method of selecting capitalization rates, 134
Employment, ideal maximum distances to place of, 38, 39

Factories (*see* Manufacturing plants)
Farm real estate:
    average value per acre, 195–209
        time adjustments for, 196
    useful lives of improvements on, 210–213
Federal Housing Administration (FHA):
    home loan data, 75, 76, 80, 81
    LUI scale, 28–34
4-3-2-1 Rule for lot depth, 58, 59

Gas stations (*see* Service stations)
Gettel Method of selecting capitalization rates, 136–139
Golf courses, supportive population needed for, 50, 51

Hoffman-Neill Rule for lot depth, 56, 57
Hoffman Rule for lot depth, 55
Hospitals, mortgage loan interest rates on, compared with other property types, 119
Hotels and motels:
    debt coverage factors on motel loans, 123
    developing new rules of thumb for, 222
    mortgage loan interest rates on motels compared with other property types, 119
    parking requirements for, 43, 44
    typical operating ratios: for major hotels and motor hotels, 163–169
        for motels, 159–162
    useful lives of buildings and furnishings, 210–213
Houses:
    best time to buy, 91–93
    depreciation tables, 214–216
    parking requirements for, 43, 44
    price indexes, 93
    Rule of 100: New, 83, 84
        Old, 81, 82
    useful lives of, 210–213

Income properties:
    debt coverage factors for, 121–123
    impact of time on, 97–99
    importance of cash flow, 104, 105
    interest rate vs. payment size, 110–115
    loan term: related to amortization, 145–147
        related to lease term, 141–143
    maximum rent for "blue chip" tenants, 148, 149
    present worth tables, 100–103
    selecting capitalization rate (*see* Capitalization rates, methods of selecting)
    typical operating ratios: for apartments, 150–152
        for major hotels and motor hotels, 163–169
        for major office buildings, 153, 154
        for motels, 159–162
        for shopping centers, 155–158
    typical percentage rents, 171–181
    useful lives of improvements, 210–213
    value of, related to general rate movements, 124–126
    variations in interest rate by property type, 117–119
    yields from, related to prime rate, 126, 127
Instant mortgage-equity technique, 134, 135
Interest rates (*see* Capitalization rates; Mortgage lending)
Irregular lots, rules for, 63–66

Johnson Method (mortgage-equity technique) for selecting capitalization rates, 134

Land:
    how long to hold, 35–37
    how much to pay for, 26, 27
Land planning:
    cost of improved lot, 12, 13
    development projections, 17–27
        financial statements for, 17–22
            of cash flow, 25
            of financial condition, 24
            of operations and capital, 23
        for undeveloped land, 26, 27
    holding period, 35–37
    lots per acre, 5–8
    LUI scale, 28–34
    maximum distances to daily activities, 38, 39

Land planning (*Cont.*):
  streets and open space, 4
  topography and use, 9–11
  25-50-25 Percent Rule, 14, 15
  20 percent allowance for streets, 3
  The Walk-Away Test, 40–42
Law of Retail Gravitation, 51*n.*
Lot rules:
  corner, 67–70
  irregular, 63–66
  (*See also* Depth rules; Plottage rules)
LUI (land-use intensity) scale, 28–34

McLaughlin Method for selecting capitaliza-
    tion rates, 134
MAI (Member, Appraisal Institute), 227
Managers (*see* Designations, professional)
Manufacturing plants:
  debt coverage factors for, 123
  mortgage loan interest rates on, compared
    with other property types, 119
  useful lives of, 210–213
Market value, assessed value as a guide to,
    194
Medical offices:
  debt coverage factors for, 123
  locations for, 186, 187
  mortgage loan interest on, compared with
    other property types, 118
  parking requirements for, 43, 44
  useful lives of, 210–213
Mortgage-equity techniques, 134, 135
Mortgage lending:
  debt coverage factors for, 121–123
  importance of payment size, 110, 111
  interest rate vs. payment size as value
    determinant, 110–115
  interest rates related to bond yields, 106–
    109
  loan term: related to amortization, 145–
    147
    related to lease term, 141–143
  mortgage loan interest rates compared
    with other rates, 124–126
  payment tables: annual constants, 114,
    115
    loan balance after given number of
      years, 146, 147
  qualifying borrowers: one-fourth of in-
    come to PITI (principal, interest, real
    estate tax, and insurance), 78–80
    Rule of 100: New, 83, 84
      Old, 81, 82
    2.5 times annual income, 75–77

Mortgage lending (*Cont.*):
  summary of income property commit-
    ments by major insurance companies,
    112, 113
  variations in interest rate by property type,
    117–119
Motels (*see* Hotels and motels)

Noise levels, 40–42
Nursing homes, mortgage loan interest rates
    on, compared with other property types,
    119

Office buildings:
  debt coverage factors for, 123
  locations for, 186, 187
  mortgage loan interest rates on, com-
    pared with other property types,
    118
  parking requirements for, 43, 44, 46, 47
  percentage rents for, 171–181
  typical operating ratios for, 153, 154
  useful lives of, 210–213
Open space:
  for streets and parks, 3–8
  topography, 10, 11

Parabolic formula for lot depth, 60, 61
Parking garage, 49
Parking lots, 43, 44
Parking space:
  for bowling centers, 43, 44
  for churches, 43, 44
  FHA guidelines for, 28–34
  400 square feet per, 45
  for general office space, 43, 44
  maximum ideal slope for, 10, 11
  for medical offices, 43, 44
  for motor hotels and restaurants, 43, 44
  in multilevel garages, 49
  residential, 43
  Urban Land Institute (ULI) parking index,
    46–48
Percent constants:
  examples of, 111–113
  explanation of, 110, 111
  related to other rates, 124–126
  tables, 114, 115
  use of, in selecting capitalization rates,
    136–139
Percentage rents, 171–181
  average, by type of store, 173

Percentage rents (*Cont.*):
  in Canadian shopping centers, 175
  lease tables, 176–181
  in U.S. shopping centers, 174
Personal property differentiated from real
    estate, 191–193
Plottage rules, 71, 72
Prime rate:
  related to other rates, 124–126
  related to real estate yields, 127
Professional designations (*see* Designa-
    tions, professional)

Real property differentiated from personal
    property, 191–193
Recreational properties (*see* Bowling cen-
    ters; Golf courses; Open space)
Reilly's Law, 51*n*.
Rents (*see* Percentage rents)
Restaurants:
  locations for, 185–187
  parking requirements for, 43, 44
  typical percentage rents for, 173, 178, 179,
    181
Rule of 100:
  New, 83, 84
  Old, 81, 82

Schools, ideal maximum distances to, 38, 39
Service stations:
  percentage rents for, 171–181
  rule of thumb for valuing, 182, 183
75-25 Rule for triangular lots, 64
Shopping centers:
  debt coverage factors for, 122
  ideal maximum distances to, 38, 39
  locations for various types of stores in,
    184–187
  mortgage loan interest rates on, compared
    with other property types, 118
  parking requirements for, 46–48
  percentage rents for, 171–181
  supportive population needed for, 50, 51
  typical operating ratios of, 155–158
65-35 Rule for triangular lots, 64
60-40 Rule for triangular lots, 64
Somers, W. A., 67
SREA (Senior Real Estate Analyst), 227

Stores:
  debt coverage factors for, 122
  locations for various types of, 184–187
  maximum rent for "blue chip" tenants,
    148, 149
  mortgage loan interest rates on, compared
    with other property types, 118
  percentage rents for, 171–181
  useful lives of, 210–213
Streets:
  development cost of, 13
  open space for, 4, 6, 8
  20 percent of land area to, 3
Summation Method of selecting capitaliza-
    tion rates, 130, 131

Topography, 9–11
Transportation:
  and maximum ideal distances to daily
    activities, 38, 39
  and parking requirements, 43, 44, 46
Triangular lots, 63–66
  75-25 Rule for, 64
  65-35 Rule for, 64
  60-40 Rule for, 64
  valuing, table for, 65
2.5 times annual income for a home, 75, 77

Urban Land Institute (ULI) parking index,
    46–48
Useful lives of buildings, 210–213

Veterans Administration, home loan data,
    81

Walk-Away Test, The, 40–42
Warehouses:
  debt coverage factors for, 123
  mortgage loan interest rates on, compared
    with other property types, 119
  useful lives of, 210–213
Wholesale Price Index, 218

Zangerle Curve, 67

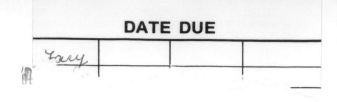

DATE DUE